Selling Antiques from Home

Selling Antiques from Home

TOM ROWLAND

General editor: Christine Brady

Pelham Books · London

First published in Great Britain by
Pelham Books Ltd
44 Bedford Square
London WC1B 3DU
1982

British Library Cataloguing in Publication Data

Rowland, Tom
    Selling antiques from home.
    1. Antiques—Purchasing
    2. Selling—Antiques
    745.1   NK1125

ISBN 0 7207 1401 X

Printed in Great Britain by Hollen Street Press Ltd, Slough
and bound by Hartnoll Ltd, Bodmin, Cornwall.

Contents

To Evelyn Hubbard
without whose help and advice this book
would not have been so comprehensive

1 Why Do You Want To Be a Dealer?

Almost everybody, at some time or other during their lifetime, gets bitten by the collecting bug. Of all the collectable things, antiques and curios are the most universally attractive and give the greatest value in pleasure and durability. There is something about all kinds of artifacts that have survived to a great age, whether they are household effects such as furniture, works of fine art or just part of the paraphernalia and ephemera of living from a bygone age, that brings out the magpie in most people.

This desire to collect the antique and curious is by no means a present-day phenomenon: indeed very little research will reveal that it has been going on for at least five hundred years. An inventory still exists from the time of the first Queen Elizabeth that records a very valuable aluminium spoon in her treasure hoard. In those days the metal was virtually unknown and considered a curiosity of great value. During the reign of Charles II the collecting of antiques and curiosities was well catered for and it is interesting to note that the pattern of dealing has hardly changed since 1650. The three leading dealers in London during Charles's reign were a Dutchman, John van Colleima, an Englishwoman, Elizabeth Genva, and a Jewish merchant, Solomon of Medina.

According to Daniel Defoe in his *Tour of Great Britain 1727* there were many dealers in china wares and lacquer. Indeed Queen Mary II was a keen collector of china and is said to have established collecting it as a hobby. 'At Hampton Court her majestys collection of Delft Ware was very large and fine. And here was also a vast stock of fine China Ware, the like whereof was not to be seen elsewhere in England. The long gallery, as above, was filled with China and every other place where it could be placed with advantage.' From Solomon of Medina Queen Mary bought in 1694 'A piece of White Atlas for £7.14.0 and a superfine Indian laquered Tronck for £27.10.0.' From van Colleima in the same year 'A pair of China Jugges £2.0.0 and a sand and ink bottle in Crystalline glass £2.0.0.'

Then, as now, the finding of a bargain was one of the chief attractions. In 1754 a Mrs Delany recorded: 'I have bought a charming old-fashioned cabinet for eight guineas that I dare say was not made for twenty.' Elsewhere there is also note of 'An Italian dealer who is pulling the wool over the eyes of the English, selling things that he gets from France and Italy for nothing at preposterous sums.'

So, having established the long history and motivation for the buying and selling of antiques and curios, let us now examine the possible reasons that make you want to become one of the cogs in that great sifting and sorting machine, the antique trade.

It is more than likely that you already collect things, perhaps a little haphazardly, acquiring here and there odd pieces of porcelain, treen, silver or embroidery that attracted your attention when you had a present to buy or were on holiday and had both time and money to spend. Perhaps you have developed a love for a particular kind of jewellery, such as Victorian jet or ornamental hatpins, and as a result are always on the lookout for a likely junk shop, an antiques fair or even another specialist with a shop where you might be able to add to your collection.

If this is the case, then one of your main reasons for wanting to become a dealer is to enable you to pursue your own interest in collecting a special kind of antique. At the same time you see that you can make a profit from selling surplus items which you have collected over the years, reinforcing these with others that have come your way during your search to expand your own collection. This profit will allow you to spend more money on your own particular collecting hobby. It will also give you more time, and a legitimate excuse, to visit antique establishments, auctions and fairs in search of suitable stock. It will provide ample opportunity to study and become an authority on your own particular branch of the antiques world.

As you become better and better known in the places where people with an interest in antiques gather, increasingly you will be approached both by dealers who have things that they think will be of interest to you and by keen collectors enquiring about things they want to buy from you. You will be well on your way to becoming a dealer.

On the other hand your motivation may be more direct. You have retired perhaps, have time on your hands and want a good excuse to get out of the house and meet new and interesting people. If you are a woman (and more women than men are well established as successful dealers in the antique trade) your children are growing up or living away from home. You now have an opportunity to get away from household chores and find a way to introduce yourself to a new environment without appearing to be pushing yourself into new company. Most likely you will also have developed an interest in antiques and now look upon this interest as providing a possible entry into a new and exciting outlet for your energy and free time.

The choice of antique dealing is a fortunate one for there are few if any more rewarding activities where you can meet a great variety of interesting and colourful people. Antique dealers and their clients are a friendly and, on the whole, helpful section of society. And the great thing about antique dealing is that you can spend as much or as little time on it as suits you and fits in with your other commitments.

Or again you may just want to make some money to augment the family budget. Times are a little hard and you do not want to see your family's standard of living slip due to inflation and rising household expenses. You have also found out the hard way that there is a lot of difference between the price at which you buy things and the price you are offered if you want, within a short time, to sell them again to raise the wind. Stop for a minute to think and you will realise that the difference between the buying and the selling price of an article is someone's profit. Think a little deeper and you will deduce that it isn't all profit — some of the difference goes on overheads, such as rent, rates, heating, transport costs and money tied up in goods that could be earning interest in a Building Society.

Particularly if you are in the latter category, it is time to pause and consider very carefully if it is wise to try your hand at establishing a business to sell antiques from home. Be warned: it is easier to lose money than to make it if you are green and inexperienced in the art of trading in antiques. You must learn the ropes first. This is a process, like most other forms of education, that takes a little time. So don't plunge in before you have tested the temperature of the water.

You must first and foremost master your subject and know what you are talking about. Obviously nobody knows all there is to know about every type of antique, but if you think your particular interest is, for instance, small silver articles or Victorian costume jewellery or collectable plates, before you venture into the hard world of buying in order to sell again, do some studying around the subject. It is just as easy to underprice a bargain as to pay too much for something that looks attractive.

If you fancy having a go at general bric-a-brac, it is even more important to both discover and memorise the prices at which the articles you are going to handle change hands. You will soon find that there is, within fairly wide limits, a correct price for almost everything. Furthermore some things are far more saleable than others and fashions change more rapidly than you would think. It only takes a well-known personality to start wearing an 'antique' hair comb or watch fob for the price to soar, only to come tumbling down in a few months, leaving the unwary with a load of unsaleable stock.

You must be able to differentiate between the genuine, the reproduction and the blatant fake. You must know the difference in value between perfect and damaged goods and be able to detect where repairs and restoration have been done. You must develop the eye of a hawk and the ability to smell out both a bargain and a stinker.

As soon as you feel that you are sufficiently equipped to take the plunge, it is time to examine the pros and cons of dealing from home. Firstly, apart from the cost of your initial stock, the overheads are virtually non-existent. As you feel your way into the trade you will find that any initial fears and doubts will fade, you will quickly gain confidence, begin to discover the things you like best to handle and generally feel at ease with trading. But you are not in any way committed to stay in the trade if you find that you don't like it.

Antique dealing can occupy as much or as little of your time as you like. You will never be tied down to regular hours when trading from home, as opposed to having a shop. In these circumstances dealing can become a stepping stone to a new career or remain a part-time hobby to provide additional interest and forge new friendships, as you wish. With growing trading experience you can appraise the things you already possess — the bits of your own collection and other items that have accumulated over the years that can form part of your initial trading stock.

Your biggest expenses are going to be transport and advertising. Transport because you will have to get around to fairs and auctions to buy and to familiarise yourself with what is going on as well as taking a stand at some of the fairs to sell your own stock. Advertising because you will need to get your name known and work up a clientele. But neither of these items need be excessively expensive in the first instance, particularly if you have the use of a car.

Any temptation to rent a shop (and you are bound to run into an opportunity to do so that seems the chance of a lifetime) should be resisted. If you are inclined to a shop, you will find that other equally attractive occasions will turn up from time to time. Renting a shop is quite a commitment. You are likely to have to sign a lease agreement for a period of years, perhaps purchase shop fittings and decorate the premises. As well as rent there is insurance, rates, heating and lighting. Experience may reveal that the shop is in a bad position. Premium sites cost big money and back street premises attract very few customers.

Once you have a shop you are tied to it. If it is not open during normal hours people will soon stop bothering to come at all so you will have to employ staff while you are away buying or doing other things. These days staff mean National Insurance as well as wages and all kinds of complications like PAYE. A shop, in short, is a full-time commitment if it is to be a success. Think very carefully before taking one on, and as far as antiques are concerned start trading from home and use other people's shops to sell your goods. We will discuss this aspect more fully later on in the book.

Let us now review the various sources of information and fountains of knowledge available to you. First of all there is a considerable variety of price guides to the trade, some very general, many highly specialised and concerned with a single group, such as Goss china or Staffordshire figures. These guides, undoubtedly useful as a *guide*, should not, however, be treated as bibles. Because of the timelag between the collection of information and publication they are, to some extent, out-of-date. Prices of any article also vary from region to region and, as any observer of auction sales will know, the price of an article can fluctuate wildly depending on who is in the auction room bidding at the time of the sale.

Price guides do nevertheless provide useful general guidance and sources of reference to even the widely experienced dealer. Details of some of these various publications are given later. They are obtainable either direct or through bookshops and some antique dealers, but don't forget that your public library will also get copies for you, if they are not already in the reference section. Make sure, too, that the books you use for reference purposes are up-to-date. Some are reprinted every year, some have a subscription up-dating service with price amendments every six months. Often at antiques fairs there is a stall selling books and guides devoted to a wide range of subjects and there are also specialist direct mail booksellers, such as The Antiques Book Centre and Stobart and Son Ltd (for addresses see page 103). Both maintain up-to-date lists of reference books, Stobart mainly on craft subjects.

One of the most rewarding sources of a broad spectrum of antiques are the antiques fairs, the village hall variety not the Park Lane Hotel or Olympia. These fairs bring together a large number of people selling a tremendous variety of goods which makes them one of the best schools of experience to learn about the trade and how it is conducted, find out about prices and make useful contacts. At these fairs the competition is fierce in many kinds of collector's items, particularly the popular ones, the keen-eyed dealers will quickly snap up any underpriced article while shrewd buyers will ignore the over-expensive.

For pure research into any aspect of antiquities, museums are the first choice. Of course you must find out which museum has a specialist collection for study and experts who will give you guidance in recognition and classification (but not values). Museums are not valuers. You will invariably find museum staff anxious to help and ready to direct your inquiries to specialists in other museums where necessary. The museum advisory services are not generally used as extensively as they could be, so you will usually find specialists keen to assist.

And, finally, there are the antiques shops themselves. You will find that they tend to congregate in areas most visited by tourists, in centres such as Camden Passage behind the Angel tube station in Islington, Portabello Market in Notting Hill Gate in London and provincial centres such as Brighton, Bath, York and the Cotswolds. Many towns have antiques centres containing the small shops of a dozen or more dealers. These locations are ideal places for concentrated study. The whole art is looking and remembering.

If by the time you have read this far you are beginning to wonder if it may not be a better idea to take up dressmaking or cookery, do not despair. The vast majority of dealers are far from being experts and you do not have to aspire to the high standards that I have suggested to start trading with every expectation of success.

I know one very old lady who throughout her entire trading life ignored all price guides and rules, bought whatever she liked and stuck between ten and fifteen per cent only on the article. Over the years she worked up such a trade that her turnover, mainly to other antique dealers in a thirty-mile radius, amounted to between two and three thousand pounds a week. Her business, still conducted from her own home which has no shop window and is in a residential street, has taken over the entire ground floor and spread into the adjoining cottage. Of course, she now knows a great deal about the antique trade and is a well-known personality in the local trade, but she still conducts her business from home where she started it over fifty years ago.

2   Buying and Selling

Getting Your Stock Together

It has been pointed out on many occasions that all dealers in antiques alternate between equally traumatic states of either having too much stock or being desperately short and not being able to find what they want at the right price.

As soon as you start dealing it will become obvious that you are going to have to invest almost as much time in searching for suitable stock as in selling it. What is more you must purchase at a price that allows you to make a reasonable profit.

As mentioned earlier, some of your initial range of things to sell may have been gleaned from your own and your family's accumulated possessions of which you have grown tired or they have been discarded into the back of a dressing-table drawer, the attic or an outhouse. These surplus possessions may add up to a useful little nucleus but hardly enough to make a big enough show on their own at the local antiques fair. You have got to get some more together and the next obvious and immediate source is your friends.

Friends

They are all going to be interested in your proposed new venture and many will be anxious to help. They may have things that they too would like to sell and, as an alternative to buying their discarded treasures, consider the possibility of selling them on their behalf. This is a particularly useful course to follow if you are short of initial capital to float your enterprise. It also has the advantage of not putting you in the embarrassing situation of having to turn down items which you consider unsuitable for your type of business. Instead you can take them on a sale-or-return basis for a month or so to see if they will sell.

At this stage you must start to be very businesslike for if you are not you will quickly lose a lot of your friends. Never rely on either your memory or theirs. *Write everything down* that you take on a S.O.R. basis in a special separate book; each item having the name and address of the owner, an accurate description of the article, the date of acceptance and of eventual sale, the price agreed and your commission. Clearly there has to be a discussion with your friend on what he or she expects to get for each item with which you are being entrusted. Almost invariably your friend's expectation of return will be higher than the article's true value, so you will have to gently talk down the price.

Before you start you will have to make up your own mind about the terms on which you will trade. You have two basic choices: (a) You agree a firm (minimum) price that your friend will receive for his (or her) article as soon as it is sold, or (b) You fix a price below which the article will not be sold and agree a percentage commission for yourself. This should not be less than twenty-five per cent if you want your business to be profitable.

If you decide on (a) you can, of course, make your own final price for the sale of the article and possibly make a higher profit — but if your friend sees the article being offered for sale at some time in the future they may be annoyed to see how much mark-up you are getting. You are going to have to explain that trade discounts are commonplace and have to be taken into account when pricing an article. More of this later.

In all events you are going to have to point out that yours, like any other business, has overheads and so you must make a fair profit. In order to avoid any awkwardness many dealers arrange to dispose of locally purchased goods to dealers outside the area, or sell them in auction.

Other dealers

However, friends with things to sell soon run out and you will quickly have to turn to other sources of supply. The first is other dealers. The whole of the antique trade may be looked upon as a huge sorting machine that classifies and redistributes other people's discarded possessions where, eventually, they will once more be either of practical use or at least be wanted for their curiosity value. As a result a great deal of trading goes on between dealers, each one looking for his or her own speciality. In fact the most exciting part of an antiques fair is often the hour or so's trading that goes on between stallholders before the doors open to the general public.

There are disadvantages to acquiring stock from other dealers. To begin with it is unlikely that you will be offered more than a ten per cent discount on the marked asking price when you put the question 'What trade can you give on this please?' You are not going to grow rich or even cover your expenses on a profit of ten per cent! In addition the article you are contemplating buying has most probably already been looked at and passed over by other dealers visiting the shop. If it has not already sold at the price marked, why should you be able to sell it for even more?

In order to buy profitably from another dealer you have got to be able to answer one or more of the following questions favourably:

1 Can I restore, clean or otherwise improve it, thus enhancing its value?

2 Can I match it up with something else already in my possession, such as a cup to a saucer or a piecrust tray to a wine table base to take two random examples?

3 Have I already got a customer who is likely to buy it from me at a handsome profit?

4 Have I spotted a bargain that the present owner has missed or, through ignorance, does not appreciate (silver snuff boxes have been passed over as base metal before now)?

5 Is the article of higher value in my area or to my clientele than it is to that of the present owner?

And the one question that you *must* be able to answer whenever you buy anything is 'Can I add on enough money when repricing it to make a worthwhile profit in a reasonably short time?'

Now you can see how valuable an asset specialised knowledge in one or two narrow fields can be. It will give you a tremendous advantage over everyone who does not possess it. I know one dealer who for years has made a good living buying only blue and white porcelain from other dealers and immediately putting these pieces into auction. So few people have his knowledge of the subject that he can always spot what they have overlooked and turn his knowledge to advantage. Another acquaintance has put together over the years a tremendously valuable list of international collectors of wine and other glasses. He only attends a dozen or so selected trade fairs a year and circulates his list of collectors every three months or so with a duplicated catalogue of what he has on offer.

Auction sales

Perhaps the very best source of stock for a beginner is to buy from auction sales. There is no need to be overawed or frightened by them, it is only unfamiliarity that provokes the misgivings. Auctioneers are in business to sell goods as efficiently and quickly as possible, not to trap the unwary into buying unwanted articles.

However, it is important to appreciate that all auction sales are not the same — indeed it is true to say that each has its own distinctive style and personality. You must get to know the idiosyncrasies of those you are going to attend regularly, and it *is* an advantage to go to a few sales regularly to get to know both the auctioneers and the regular attenders. In the first instance go to several auctions in both your nearest big town and a country area to look and listen. Don't get carried away and start bidding for things which

18

look like the chance of a lifetime — there are three to four hundred chances every week in hundreds of rooms all over the country.

You will quickly discover that some rooms have regular sales of general household goods with a sprinkling of antiques throughout. Some save up the better antique material and hold a special sale every couple of months, some specialise only in high-quality lots, sending the more mundane to another branch or even another auctioneers.

Many rooms separate the goods on offer into categories: the kitchen equipment and garden tools first, then household sundries followed by furniture, carpets, pictures, silver and small 'showcase' items. The bigger auctioneers at the top end of the market have sales devoted entirely to specialities, such as silver every week, carpets once a month down to pot lids twice a year. Such arrangements allow specialists to attend only those parts of a sale dealing with their particular interest.

As you grow more familiar with the workings of each auction room, you will find that each auctioneer has his own characteristic style. Some work at a spanking pace, selling one hundred and twenty or more lots an hour; some get through only seventy or eighty lots in the same time. You can judge the time when the lot that interests you is likely to come up if you know your auctioneer. You will also start to recognise the dealers and spot the methods employed by them and the auctioneer for making and taking bids. In other words the habits of the regulars, how much of a sense of humour the man with the hammer has and the general atmosphere that the room creates.

There is, in fact, no chance that you may scratch your ear and find that you have bought a Victorian mangle. The auctioneer will take a first bid from two or more known buyers and continue to advance the price of the bids until he is given a sign that the buyer has ceased bidding. This explains why sometimes the bids seem to be coming from the lamp brackets. He will not take a bid from a stranger without making certain that a bid is intended and after you have bought a lot the auctioneer will ask your name if he does not know you.

When you have found one or two auction rooms where you feel at home, and that regularly offer the kinds of goods you want, start attending the sales and get known there. Ask to have catalogues of forthcoming sales sent to you. Most rooms charge for their catalogues and postage, but if you become a regular buyer you may find the service becomes a free one.

Mark the catalogues in advance, noting the lots that seem as if they might be of interest and then go along on viewing day, or before the sale starts, and inspect very carefully the lots you have marked. If you can't find them one of the porters will willingly help. If you feel confident to do so make a note of the top price you are prepared to pay beside each lot. When the lot comes up don't be afraid to go one or two bids over your price, but on no account get carried away by the excitement of the moment. There is nothing worse than coming away from an auction with a feeling of regret that something you desperately wanted might have been yours for one more pound.

Do make sure that the auctioneer knows you are bidding. Shout or wave your programme if necessary to register your first bid. After that the auctioneer will take your bid in turn with the other punters, literally on the nod, until you intimate that you have ceased bidding by shaking your head or otherwise signing off. And when you return home from your auction, if you have viewed carefully and bid within your limit you shouldn't suffer too often from the dreadful sinking feeling known to all dealers of finding a crack in the Worcester teapot, a drawer broken in the davenport or a ruby missing from a ring.

There is, of course, a lot more to be learned about auction sales. We will discuss some more of the points later on.

The 'runner'

A little-known source of stock items, except that is to the antique trade itself, is the runner. These people, almost invariably men, are the most interesting breed of people in the antique world. They are generally welcome callers, except on the days when you have no money to spare for buying and one turns up with the bargain you must have at all costs.

These traders do not have shops of their own but buy anything they think they can make a profit on from any source they can find. They normally work on a very small profit margin, relying on turning their estate car or van load of stock over quickly, sometimes twice a day. Some runners have been in the trade for years and are both reliable and honest. Some are a bit fly-by-night, turning up a couple of times then to be seen no more. Obviously caution is called for until you get to know your runners: you don't want to find yourself landed with stolen property.

But how do you get to know them? With a shop it is relatively easy because they will come to find you. You will often see them around antique fairs and in other people's antique shops, with their plastic carrier bags or samples of their current best buy. Have a quiet word with them and tell them where you can be contacted. Also tell them the things you will be most interested in buying − they are all good at buying for specific customers. Make your contact discreetly so as not to offend the owner of the shop − dealers guard their pet runners most jealously and are not anxious to share them with you.

In passing, note the fact that running for the antiques trade is one of the options open to you in dealing from home.

Other sources

Almost in the same category as runners are dustmen and 'totters' who rake over rubbish dumps. The way people throw away valuables is a continual source of amazement and dustmen are, of course, aware of this and get first pick as part of their perks. They will sell everything of value that they retrieve to whoever pays the best price. So approach your dustman and be prepared to pay him a fair price for what he brings, and do take everything he turns up with — if you don't want some of it, the next runner will buy it from you.

A few years ago a gipsy I used to know came and offered me a set of six late Regency chairs which he had managed to balance precariously on his bike. It emerged that he had found them discarded on the local rubbish tip and I was foolish enough to offer him a large enough sum for him to refuse, and hawk them around for the best price he could get. A few weeks later I saw the same chairs, badly restored, for sale in a nearby town at twice the price I had offered. They turned up again, by now properly restored, in a top dealer's window in Kensington, priced at over a thousand pounds. I wonder what the owner who threw them onto the dump would say if he knew.

Jumble sales are also a potentially good source of certain kinds of stock, such as occasional furniture in need of renovation, china ornaments and bric-a-brac. If you are catering for collectors of old kitchen implements, buttons, ancient garments or the like, jumble sales are worth visiting, but don't expect to find valuable pieces very often. Organisers are usually too knowledgeable to let good stuff slip through undetected and will have anything they think may be worth a good price valued by a tame dealer or auctioneer.

You can occasionally buy very well from little old ladies who get to know about you and pop in with newspaper-wrapped treasures in carrier bags. But, again, be on your guard against the legion of little old ladies who try to sell you the family heirlooms which, in fact, they bought yesterday at the local jumble sale.

Be cautious too over members of the public who, quite honestly, believe that an article they are offering to you is

22

'more than a hundred years old, and belonged to grandma'. More than likely it will turn out to be no earlier than 1900 to 1920. You see grandma was eighty when she died and she gave it to mum who is sixty-two now. What has been overlooked is the fact that most likely grandma was forty or so when she bought or was given the article in question, and mum was fifteen at the time. When you work it out each generation is separated by only twenty or twenty-five years if you calculate from the normal age of bearing children.

On the few occasions that a little old lady really has something to sell that is of considerable value, do settle on a fair price. It is likely that the money is genuinely needed and you don't want her on your conscience. What is more you want her to come back with the rest that she will want to sell at some time in the future. A good local reputation for fair dealing will go a long way to ensuring that you have first pick of whatever there is on offer. A reputation — either good or bad — spreads like a stubble fire.

If you feel up to taking them on, house clearances can be gold mines. In consequence there is usually considerable competition among dealers who specialise in this type of trading. The usual way to get house clearances is to advertise regularly in the classified columns of your local paper and to make yourself known to estate agents and solicitors in your immediate area. The deal is that you purchase the entire contents of the home of (usually) a deceased owner from their heirs or legal representatives.

The first thing to do is view the house and establish *exactly* what you are being allowed to purchase. It is a favourite trick for the relatives to agree to the sale of contents and then decide that after all they will take with them just those articles that you wanted and on which you based your tendered price, leaving behind the junk. The safest thing to do, if you can, is to start to clear as soon as you have agreed a price, removing the most important items immediately. Do not start making inventories, if you do you are inviting the new owners to start haggling over the price again because they will be surprised to find the full extent of the contents.

Before the dustmen call, empty out the dustbins. You will be surprised how people are inclined to have a little tidy-up before calling you in and, in their ignorance, throw away some of the most interesting bits and pieces, like old watches that don't work (but have 9ct gold cases) or rosewood tea caddies with their hinges broken and some veneer chipped off. It is not easy for the amateur to differentiate between real junk and potential small treasures.

Your contract will most likely be to clear the house completely and sweep out the rooms. This is heavy, dirty work and you will earn your money if you take the job on. You will most likely have to burn the unsaleable residues of junk, dump the unburnable at the nearest corporation tip and put into auction all the old furniture and kitchen equipment of no use to you as stock.

Now, having explained the main sources of stock, a critical analysis of what and how to buy will not be wasted. There is no school like experience, and unfortunately everyone has to make their own mistakes and pay for them. It is essential to develop a quick eye to spot anything with potential that can be cleaned, renovated or otherwise improved. These are the items that will show you the highest profit margins for, when presentable, they will contain a large element of your own labour for which you can charge in addition to the normal profit.

This critical eye must also be highly selective. Knowing what things are likely to sell quickly and what is likely to stick is most important. You can very easily come to the end of your capital resources by buying beautiful and highly priced goods that may take months to sell, and there is nothing more demoralising than waiting for the right wealthy customer to come along. Money on the shelf is money tied up when it should be earning you a profit.

By all means have a few glamorous and eye-catching

pieces for 'window dressing' which will add style to your business, but reinforce these show pieces with bread and butter items which sell for modest prices and will contribute to a steady turnover of stock.

At some stage or other you will have to consider catering for specialist collectors and find an unexploited, or more likely under-exploited, section of the market. This is a vast subject and guidance on what to specialise in is beyond the scope of this book, but suffice it to say that inspite of the large number of people engaged in selling antiques there are still areas of the collectable left to be exploited. Who in 1939 when cigarette companies ceased printing cigarette cards would have believed that the trade in them would be even larger nearly half a century later?

Dealing in a specialist area leads you deeper into taking commissions from friends and regular customers to buy on their behalf. Like everything else, there are snags here. We all know the story of the man who commissioned a friend to buy him a shaggy dog. It had to be very large, grey in colour with blue eyes and a very long tail. After months of searching the friend found a dog that matched the specification in every detail and brought the animal back in triumph to the man who took one look at it and said: 'I don't want one that's *that* shaggy.'

The same thing happens when buying antiques on commissions: you can rarely be certain that your customer will buy what you have found for them. He or she may be short of money at the time, may have found the same thing somewhere else or have a dozen other different reasons for refusing to buy. But such disappointments are not the end of the world — another customer is bound to turn up.

You must also avoid the very common pitfall of wanting to keep for your own collection all the best bits you find. The temptation, I know, is often overwhelming but it must be resisted. If you want your business to thrive and prosper, you must give your customers a chance to snap up some of the plums.

Finally, a few hints on how much to charge, which is closely allied with how much to pay. When buying anything for resale the only important question to ask yourself is 'How much do I think I can sell it for?' The difference between that figure and the price you pay has got to cover your petrol, and other car expenses like tyres, insurance, licence, servicing and eventual replacement, all your overheads, like the rental of stands at fairs, advertising, printing, and after all that show you some profit to live on. (Thank goodness you don't have as many overheads as shopkeepers.)

We already know that you are not going to get much more than ten per cent discount when buying from another dealer, so when you do you have to be certain that you can put quite a lot on top of the present retail price. Fortunately this is often possible — what sells well in Manchester won't sell at all in Bolton. The mark-up you require, that is overheads plus profit, will vary considerably. Unfortunately there is no rule of thumb, except that it should be as much as the article can carry without making it a non-seller.

Quite a number of people run an antique business for the pleasure and company that they derive from it, rather than purely for gain. They are content with a very low cash return on the hours that they put in. You are going to ignore them for here we are discussing a profitable business venture.

As a general rule you should aim at making between thirty and fifty per cent gain on everything you sell. On articles of high value — say anything over £50.00 — you may find that you can only make fifteen or twenty per cent. On articles of low value the reverse is true and you may often make one hundred per cent, or even more.

You must also understand something about how percentages work, if you are going to work on percentage margins. If you find them muddling you can work purely on intuition; but you must keep an idea of a realistic margin of profit in your head. Study the calculations below carefully and you will see how percentages work and the difference between an added percentage and a deducted percentage. (Where 30% is referred to, the exact figure is 33⅓% or one third.)

PROFIT

Cost of article	Percentage	Add on	Selling price
£12.00	+10%	£1.20	£13.20
£12.00	+30%	£4.00	£16.00
£12.00	+50%	£6.00	£18.00

DISCOUNT

Marked price	Percentage	Subtract	Selling price
£13.20	-10%	£1.32	£11.88
£16.00	-30%	£5.33	£10.67
£18.00	-50%	£9.00	£9.00

You see 30% added on is a lot different from 30% taken off. A good rule of thumb to remember is that 50% on = 30% off. Do it yourself.

$$£12+50\% = £18 - 30\% = £12.$$

Another very sound practice is to mark on the reverse of your pricing label a coded price below which you cannot afford to sell if you are to avoid making a loss. Here is one simple example:

T.G.P. ROWLAND
1 2 3 4 5 6 7 8 9 0

So £12 becomes TG and £3.25 P-GO.

Antiques Fairs

There is no doubt that one of the most important aspects of trading from home is participation in some at least of the many antiques fairs that are held in church halls, hotel functions rooms, exhibition halls and other meeting places throughout the country. They are an extremely useful way of getting to know people in the antique trade and of buying new stock as well as, hopefully, making money.

Let us first examine the different kinds, or perhaps more accurately the different standards of antiques fairs to be found in various parts of the country (and indeed abroad). Starting at the top there are the National and International antiques fairs. These are usually held in National Exhibition Centres or prestigious venues such as Olympia or the Royal Academy where Burlington House Antiques Fair is sometimes held. Occasionally major hotels like Grosvenor House or the Washington Hotel host these outstanding events.

These occasions go on for ten days or a fortnight, they attract top international dealers as well as many smaller specialists with an international clientele and are attended by many thousands of connoisseurs and collectors prepared to spend thousands, even tens of thousands of pounds on a single item. But they are not all glamour – like the top auction rooms, Sothebys and Christies, the majority of transactions are much more modest. Nevertheless, these fairs are not for the beginner.

A little down the league are the provincial antiques fairs that are usually also staged for about a week in hotel suites or public halls. Here too the organisers provide the shells of stands of various sizes and attract as stallholders dealers from all over the area. These fairs, like the national ones, have a panel of judges who vet everything offered for sale and impose a 'dateline'. That is a minimum age for all the antiques displayed, which is normally as follows:

Furniture	Pre-1830
Glass, metalware, porcelain, silver, silver plate and clocks	Pre-1860
Jewellery and Oriental carpets	Pre-1890

Pictures and carriage
clocks   Pre-1900

Of somewhat less importance are two- or three-day fairs
which have less rigorous conditions imposed on the
exhibitors.

And, finally, of paramount interest to the beginner, are
the table-top fairs, held for one day only and open to anyone who wants to sell anything collectable that can be
vaguely described as more or less old. These fairs, too, can
be subdivided. There are the commercial ones run by professional organisers who know what they are doing,
advertise the event adequately in local newspapers,
local radio and fly posting, lay out the stalls so that both
stall-holders and the general public have reasonable
access.

The other kind are the fairs organised by different kinds
of charity groups, such as a church restoration fund or a
local hospital appeal. These are probably, though not
necessarily, less well organised due to lack of experience,
are often less well advertised so draw fewer potential
buyers and may even provide stallholders with inadequate
and inequitable table area to display their wares properly.

In spite of the occasional lack of experience (I once attended one where the person who arranged the tables for-
got that the stallholders had to get in and out and pushed
the tables together, the only access being to crawl beneath
the table), these charity fairs can be great fun and are
usually less expensive than the commercial ones. The great
thing about them is that the food is almost always superb,
being home cooked by a bevvy of devoted ladies, so you
need not bother to take along sandwiches and a flask of
coffee, as is advisable at commercial fairs where the food is
usually expensive and the coffee foul.

Most table-top fairs take place on either a Saturday or
Sunday and may include handicrafts and produce. You
should, however, stick strictly to antiques at all times if you

wish to build up a reputation, and above all keep strictly clear of reproductions of any kind.

These days the definition of what is genuinely antique has become somewhat blurred. The datelines quoted above are those generally accepted by the majority of the trade, but for export and Customs Duty purposes anything over one hundred years old, or in some cases anything over fifty years old, is considered antique enough to enter another country duty-free. In table-top fairs, though, where what are classed by the trade as 'smalls' are generally offered for sale, one often sees items that look to be no older than a decade or so.

The cost of taking a stall at an antiques fair varies considerably — from £5.00 to £15.00 for a six-foot frontage at a table-top fair to £5.00 to £15.00 per square foot of floor space for those at the top end. This means that a small stand ten feet by ten feet could cost over a thousand pounds against seven pounds fifty for the average table-top fair!

When you are first starting out the problem is, of course, to find out where the fairs are being held and how you book a stall. If you wait until a fair is advertised to the general public you most likely are too late to secure a place, and may have to wait until next year to get in. It is certainly not easy to get a stall at antiques fairs in some parts of the country and good fairs are inclined to have a long waiting list. You have to feel your way and wait your turn.

The best answer, if you can, is to make friends with someone already in the trade and find out from them the names of organisers and the dates of forthcoming fairs. You might even be lucky and find someone who will share their stall with you, or let you come in to assist them. Failing this you should take out a subscription to one or two of the specialist antiques journals. These are not normally to be found on bookstalls, except for a few like the *Connoisseur*, and at all events a subscription to some of them will keep you in touch with what is going on in the trade and, in the best of them, the trend in prices.

A well grouped and attractive show of pottery, porcelain and glass with a cabinet of silver.

Of the twenty-odd magazines and publications produced on the subject in this country, possibly the three most useful for advance information about both antiques fairs and auction sales are the *Antique Finder*, published monthly except August by Antique Finder Ltd, 5 Church Street, Woodbridge, Suffolk (Tel. 03943 5501), the *Antiques Trade Gazette*, published by Metropress Ltd, 116 Long Acre, London WC2E 9PA (Tel. 01-240 5735), issued weekly on Wednesdays and *Art and Antiques Weekly*, published by Independent Magazines Ltd, 181 Queen Victoria St, London EC4V 4DD (Tel. 01-405 7340).

At this stage, having collected information about the dates and venues of convenient local antiques fairs, you have got to decide how many you wish to attend as a stallholder. Some dealers from home go to as many as one a fortnight, averaging twenty or more fairs a year, some

Good use of spotlights. These items will really catch the potential buyer's eye.

attend only three or four, sticking to those in their immediate area or all the fairs arranged by a single organiser. Certainly at the most popular fairs you are likely to have to wait for someone to drop out before you can obtain a place, but the biggest fairs may have as many as a hundred stalls so a chance to obtain one will not entail a very long wait. Once you find the fairs that most suit you, you will be wise to book forward from fair to fair or year to year.

Before booking yourself a stall or table at a fair find out from the organisers all the essential things you need to know:

1 The time of opening, usually from 10 or 10.30 am to 4.30 or 5.00 pm.
2 The rent and what you get for it (usually no more than a two or two-and-a-half metre (six or eight foot) tressle table and a couple of chairs).
3 The location and size of the stall. Have you a back wall

32

that you can use?

4 Whether food and drinks are available.

5 Where and how the fair is being advertised.

6 How the hall is being lighted and the availability of an electric point.

7 Car parking and unloading and loading facilities.

The lighting of a stand is of considerable importance and will greatly influence the volume of your sales at many fairs. If you can, go and have a look at the hall in advance and find out the location of your pitch. If you can secure the use of an electric point, take your own additional lighting, particularly if you are dealing in jewellery and silver — it never looks good in a dark unlit corner.

If all else fails take along candles and as many attractive candelabra as you can russle up. On a winter's afternoon a candlelit stall is very attractive and will draw customers.

Now that you are booked up to attend a fair you need to spend some time making preparatory arrangements of the things you are going to take with you.

First, a suitable *table covering*. This should be either white or a plain dark colour. Too bright or boldly patterned a background detracts attention from the stock displayed on it.

Second, always take a small *card table* (and cloth). There may be room for it either beside or even in front of your stall and this will increase your display area. You may not be able or allowed to use it but it takes up very little space in the car and does not hurt to have it along.

Third, a *notebook*, each page headed with the place and date of the fair. In this you will keep a detailed log, entering a description of each item sold and the price. At the end of the day's trading write down the total of your turnover. This book is invaluable for comparison of what kind of things sell best at which fair, and local preferences do vary considerably. It will also remind you if you have never taken more than, say, £20 at this venue that the effort in this case is not warranted and that this is a fair to give a miss

This stall is well attempted, but the result is not very attractive.

when it comes round next time. Do not be too hasty in your judgment, however, it may be that you had the wrong stock or just that it was a bad day. (Don't forget a pencil or Biro.)

Fourth, *tissue paper* and *sellotape* for doing up parcels, at any rate for the better and more delicate things. A tidy parcel will impress your customer favourably and maybe he or she will come back or become a regular.

Fifth, *newspapers* to wrap bulkier and breakable things. Newspapers are the great universal packing and protecting material of the antique dealer.

Sixth, *labels and tags* to price and describe your goods. Even if you have carefully priced and labelled everything before setting out you may want to change things or label new stock acquired before the fair opens.

Seventh, plenty of *change* in both coin and pound notes. You are bound to start off by having a customer who only has a ten pound note. The most efficient and secure way of carrying your money and having it immediately to hand is a strong canvas apron with a zip-fastened double pocket. This is better than cash boxes or purses which can easily be mislaid or even stolen.

All these things can be put into a nice big flat-bottomed basket along with your sandwiches, flask of coffee, spectacles, keys, chequebook and anything else that is essential to survival over a long, gruelling day. A friend's husband insists that a bottle of red plonk goes with him to any fair he attends. Any friendly neighbouring dealer is made even friendlier by the offer of a glass of wine at lunchtime.

And finally, your *stock*, not forgetting your stall fittings. As far as stock is concerned, the choice is yours. No more guidance can be given than in general terms. It should be compact enough to be easily transported and it should have amongst it one or two show pieces (some dealers will keep back good pieces for forthcoming shows). Most beginners start off with a mixed range of stock including some ceramics (mostly ornaments and decorative plates), a range

Well arranged, but short of stock? Why not use the silent butlers on the right for display too?

of small boxes and caddies made of a variety of materials (wood, spelter, antimony, ivory etc), a mixture of small silver and EPNS pieces, some brass and copper, maybe a few pieces of carved wood, watches and clocks, dolls and dolls clothes, instruments both musical and scientific, certainly glass and old toys, needlework, jewellery — the list is endless. The things not normally seen at one-day fairs but only at the more prestigious gatherings are large pieces of furniture. The type of customer patronising table-top fairs does not expect to see, or come prepared to buy, bulky items.

As to stall furnishings, the shop fittings as it were, you need to collect together suitable sets of small, free-standing shelves and glass display cabinets to exhibit your wares. Nothing looks worse than a flat table covered with a motley assortment of odds and ends. When erected your stall should look as similar as possible to a well-dressed shop window — except for the plate glass front — for indeed that is just what it is. Before you start a good idea is to have a dummy run and lay out your stall on the kitchen table to see how it looks.

All your stock should be transported in robust cardboard boxes, each item securely wrapped in several layers of newspaper. It is wise to separate breakables from heavy metal or stone items. You can get boxes from the nearest supermarket; get them as large as you can manage but not too heavy or bulky for you to carry from the car park to the hall in which the fair takes place. If you are completely organised you will number the cartons in the order you want to unpack them.

On the morning of the fair give yourself plenty of time to get set up, particularly if you are at an unfamiliar location. If the fair begins at 10.30 am the organisers may well let the trade visitors in at ten o'clock, so you should aim at being completely set up and ready for business at 9.30. Trade buyers can then see your stock displayed to its best advantage and also you have the chance for a quick look at other people's stock. You should try therefore to be in the hall by

A well laid out stall with good use of the stage to show small furniture.

8.30 or 9.00 am, depending on how long it takes to set up your goods. It is quite common for the hour or so before the fair opens properly to be the most profitable time of the whole day. Many out-of-town buyers make a point of combing small fairs for suitable pieces for their own shops.

At any fair two things are essential for success. One is having the right stock in the right place at the right price — only experience can teach you this. The second is to have a well-developed sense of presentation and display. If you don't sell anything all day your stock is probably over-priced and if you sell everything to other dealers before the general public is allowed into the hall then, oh dear, you were too cheap, weren't you! But don't despair, you have taken some money and bought some worthwhile ex-perience.

At most charity fairs there is a stall run by the organisers

37

which is given over to antiques and 'white elephants', donated in aid of the church tower restoration fund or whatever. Here is another good reason for getting set up early. You will be surprised at how eagerly the dealers gather like vultures round those stalls and how quickly they snap up the bargains.

You will find that if you haven't already got a good sense of display it will develop automatically when you have done several fairs. If you have small pieces of silver and jewellery then a display case or glass-fronted tray of some sort is absolutely essential, both for presentation and to protect your goods from the light-fingered person who, unfortunately, is always about.

Some dealers are so convinced of the importance of presentation that they carry with them the kind of velvet-covered stepped display unit that you see in jewellers' windows. This allows them to build up a display of their stock to maximum advantage. When lit by two or more anglepoise lamps such a display can be crowd-attracting. It goes without saying that the bigger things, like oil lamps

A good secure display of jewellery and small silver.

and dolls, must go at the back and for greatest impact a grouping of similar items produces a focus for the eye. So arrange your copper and brass in a clump, lit by a spotlight; all the blue and white ceramics together as another focal point; and separate clumps of articles with as much space between as you can spare to create centres of interest.

Now that your stall is laid out to your satisfaction you have the opportunity to wander around. But you also have the problem of keeping an eye on your own stock at all times. If it is at all possible, take a friend with you to share the job of minding the shop. Doing a fair constitutes a long, long day and you will need some time off to eat your meal, have a drink and a trip to the loo.

Certainly your next door neighbour will keep an eye on things for you while you are away and no doubt you will do the same in reciprocation, but sharing a day between two of you makes it much more enjoyable and a breath of air outside a stuffy hall every now and again helps to fend off headaches.

As far as security goes the rule is don't trust anyone. Thieves don't look like thieves and it is dreadfully depressing to find that you have had something stolen. Not only have you probably lost your day's profit because you have to allow for the value of the stolen object, but the shock of having something stolen spoils your day and leaves you with a tendency to view everyone with suspicion. You must learn not to be distracted at busy fairs. For instance a favourite trick is for one thief to engage you in conversation while the accomplice steals from the other end of the table.

One essential part of dealing at fairs is developing an ability to cope with several people at once, probably trying to sell to one person with the offer of a reduction in price while at the same time wrapping up an already sold article and giving change to a third customer. Antique fairs, like wars, consist of long periods of boredom interspersed with brief periods of intense activity.

Securing a prime position in any fair is an obvious goal,

but when you are a newcomer you will be glad to secure a position anywhere. Once you are a regular stallholder, however, as people fall out you will be able to improve your position. When you have graduated to one of the better sites, stay put. You will find that, as you become established, you will attract regular customers who will look for you in the same place at each fair. There is, therefore, no advantage in chopping and changing all the time, but when the real prime position falls vacant, grab it and hang on to it.

It is common sense to stay on good terms with both organisers and other stallholders, although this is not always easy due to conflicting interests. Be careful not to exceed your allotted space by letting your goods stray over into the area allotted to a neighbour. Be considerate and avoid embarrassing other exhibitors. They may not say anything to you, but will resent your being so inconsiderate.

If, on the other hand, someone's stall overflows onto yours be polite when pointing out the incursion into your preserve. A mild reproach is far better than an onslaught and that way you remain on good terms. Only as a last resort complain to the organiser; you have got to sit next to your neighbours all day and it is much better to live on amicable terms if you can. Fortunately most people are reasonable and only occasionally will you meet with unpleasantness.

We have spent quite a lot of time examining fairs because they are very important, particularly to the new dealer who is trying to get established and make as many contacts as possible. They are by no means the only method of trading; many dealers never exhibit at them. We will look at other methods of selling in the next chapter.

Auctions and Relations with The Trade
Buying in auction has been discussed in some detail in the

last chapter but what has already been said is only half the story, for the workings of them may seem puzzling until you understand fully what is going on under the surface.

Auction rooms should be regarded as one of the most useful sources of buying and as agencies for selling, not only to be used as a last resort. Certainly it is not wise to put goods into auction shortly after offering them all around the trade.

Each auction room has its own personality and their terms of trading are likely to vary too. For instance, they do not all charge the same rates of selling commission. Most of the smaller country auctioneers now charge the *seller* fifteen per cent on the price at which the hammer comes down, although there are still some quite important auction rooms where only ten per cent is charged.

Because of increasing overheads such as rates, heating and wages, many of the medium-size and bigger rooms now charge a *buyer's premium* to the customer in addition to a seller's commission. This may be anything from five to ten per cent and it is, of course, very important to take it into consideration if you are the buyer. As a result of being certain of a payment of, say, ten per cent from the buyer, the auctioneer will only charge six per cent in most cases to any dealer who is selling, providing he asks. Lower selling commissions are also negotiable to private customers if they have prestigious or high value property to dispose of. In auction rooms where a buyer's premium is charged it means that you have to add the percentage to the price bid when the hammer falls. For example if you bid £9.00 for an article it is in fact going to cost you £9.90 if the premium is ten per cent.

As a general rule it is wise to use country auction rooms for selling all but the most important and specialised goods. It cuts down on such costs as transportation and you will get your money very much quicker as the wait for goods to get into London auctions is about three months, and then you wait another month for the cheque to arrive.

PASKELL AND CANN

Auctioneers, Valuers, Surveyors, Estate Agents

11 - 14 EAST HILL, COLCHESTER, CO1 2QX

Telephone : 7 0 4 9 2 / 3   V.A.T. Registration No. 102 9402 12

Edward Dove, F.S.V.A.
Claude Polley, F.S.V.A.
Richard Polley, F.S.V.A.
Robert Putt, F.S.V.A.

STATEMENT OF SALE

AUCTION No. C   2581

HELD ON   17th February 1981

LOT		PRICES REALISED		SALE EXPENSES		
121	35in Oak Gateleg Table on turned legs	40		Commission 15%	ᒪ	
122	Spleter Equestrian Figure	u\s		Buying-in Fee 5% *Wanted.*		90
				V.A.T.		
				Removal Expenses		
				Contra A/c.		
				to Balance	33	10
	Total	40		**Total**	40	.

A further charge that must be borne in mind is VAT. When an auctioneer sells articles belonging to a private individual or a small trader whose turnover is low enough to exclude him or her from liability to the tax, the only VAT payable is on the auctioneer's commission. However, if the lot is being sold on behalf of a VAT registered person or company, some auction rooms now charge VAT on top of the bid price at the current rate (at the time of writing 15%). They will always make this fact quite clear when selling any lot liable to the tax.

When you are selling through auction rooms you will find that your statement will be made up showing the price received for each lot with a grand total of the several items sold on your behalf. Then at the bottom there is a small sum showing the total commission deducted plus the VAT on the commission and any other charges, such as transport, advertising, insurance etc.

So when buying or selling at auction find out first of all:

1 The commission charged to the seller,
2 The buyer's commission, if any,
3 If any lot you might buy is subject to VAT,
4 If there are any additional charges, eg insurance,
5 If there is a minimum commission charge that will affect small value lots.

It is quite normal for a seller to impose a cash limit below which he instructs the auctioneer not to sell. This is known as the 'reserve' and is properly kept confidential. When selling reserve price lots the auctioneer will not usually disclose the fact and will start to take bids in the normal way. If only one person is bidding, or in order to stimulate others to join in, the auctioneer may take fictitious bids 'off the chandelier'. This is a perfectly legitimate practice, he is only bidding the price up to reach the reserve. But if you detect that this is happening it is best to stop bidding and approach the auctioneer after the sale to try and negotiate a price below the reserve. That is a private treaty sale.

If you are the seller and the lot does not reach its reserve it is usual for a reduced commission to be charged, usually 2½% of the reserve price, with the option of putting the lot into the next sale, often with a reduced reserve or even without one at all. In this case most auctioneers will waive any commission charge for the first sale.

In many auction rooms an estimate of the probable price that each lot will fetch is available as a guide to would-be purchasers. Even in rooms where no estimate sheet is available you can usually obtain an idea of the likely price that any item will fetch. If you are seeking some guidance you should avail yourself of this service.

If for some reason you cannot attend a sale in which there are one or more lots that you would like to have, you can always leave instructions with the commission clerk, or in smaller rooms with the auctioneer or one of the porters. They will bid on your behalf. This is a valuable service much used by dealers whose time is limited. Obviously you have to tell whoever is going to bid on your behalf how much you are prepared to pay for each lot, and it must be the maximum you are willing to go to. The immediate dilemma is that if your limit is too low someone else will get it, if too high you fear that the maximum is the price you will have to pay. The latter is not necessarily the case. It is a matter of knowing and trusting your agent.

Usually *commissions,* as they are called, are left with several members of an auction room's staff and often the auctioneer will open the bidding on a lot by announcing that he has a bid of £X on the lot. All that he is doing is to announce the lowest of several bids he has noted on his order of sale. By the way, it is usual to tip the porter if he has bid on your behalf but not the auctioneer.

Because so many items pass through the hands of auctioneers every week, they are invariably the best informed people as to the current value of almost any article and in consequence it is always sensible to consult them. Most professional auctioneers are also valuers and will do valua-

44

tions for you, for which they are entitled to charge a fee. If, however, you are considering selling the goods through their rooms the valuation will be free, as will an opinion on the odd single item.

Auctioneers, on the whole, are extremely friendly and helpful people so do not hesitate to seek their advice. The larger auction houses, like most museums, have experts in specialised fields who can give guidance in the authentication and dating of articles.

The antique trade has more than its fair share of colourful characters. Indeed some may feel that half the pleasure of the trade is the variety of personalities you rub shoulders with all the time. Of course some are bad, some are bent and some are sailing close to the wind, but most are kind and helpful if you treat them in the right way. Among the most common transgressors of the law are 'the ring'. This is a group of dealers who refrain from bidding against each other in the auction room and after the sale hold their own private knock-out auction in the pub round the corner, dividing the proceeds equally amongst themselves. What they are doing, of course, is to rob the owner of the goods of the true market price.

Rings operate in many auction rooms, they are virtually impossible to stop but a combination of reserve prices, the vigilance of the auctioneer in protecting the interests of his clientele and bidding by dealers who refuse to participate in the ring will normally render them ineffective. The private buyer can always outbid them as well as he wants the goods to keep, while they want them to sell again at a profit.

The other somewhat less-than-reputable figures in the antique trade are those 'knockers' (itinerant traders who knock on doors) who pray on old people and those who are unaware of the true value of their possessions. Not all of them are disreputable, but it has become an unsavoury way of earning a living. On the other hand, the well-established and trusted dealer who trades from home and who has built up a reputation for paying fair prices is performing a true service to the community.

When you are asked by people for your opinion you will quickly find that not every other old oil painting is a Constable or a Gainsborough and all that glistens is not gold, or even Pinchbeck. Considerable tact has to be exercised to advise the proud owner that, although their family heirloom is of great sentimental value to them, it is perhaps not quite as valuable as they had hoped. You will soon learn, too, that in general the modern and unsaleable is in the sitting-room and the real valuables in the cellar, attic or outhouses, discarded as being of no real value or out of fashion, or even just broken or scratched.

Never be afraid to admit it when you are confronted with something about which you are unsure. Most people appreciate the fact that nobody can be an expert on everything and they respect a frank admission of ignorance. But by all means say that you will find out for them − if it is possible for you to do so. Never, never try to bluff your way through; you could easily be talking to an expert and it is embarrassing to find that you are being led into a trap.

When you are in someone else's shop or examining their goods at a fair, be very careful not to belittle or otherwise pour gratuitous criticism on their possessions. Some dealers seem to revel in pulling to pieces anything they see in antique shops, levelling doubts of authenticity on furniture, pointing out defects, either obvious or imagined, and generally running down and pouring scorn on everything they see. In some cases this is a ploy to try and obtain a larger discount, often it appears to be no more than common or garden spite. Such tactics are rarely successful.

These are pitfalls to avoid if you want to stay on good terms with other members of the trade. This, of course, is only common sense, but be on your guard and avoid dropping bricks. Everyone responds favourably to a bit of praise and unfavourably to bitchy criticism.

Antiques, like all other goods offered for sale, are subject to the Trade Descriptions Act, so care must be exercised

46

when describing either in writing or verbally, any article that you are trying to sell. If you sell a placed fruit bowl saying that it is Sheffield plate and it turns out to be EPNS you could easily be in trouble. Many buyers will want to have an exact description of their purchase. including its approximate age. On important articles a certificate of authenticity may be asked for. The rule is, under no circumstances give a certificate or otherwise describe an article if you are not sure about it. If you don't know, say so. And in passing remember that goods offered in auction do not come under the Act so they do not bear any guarantee of authenticity.

3 Starting the Business

Time to Get Known

When you are starting out on a career as a dealer in antiques it is important to spread the word as widely and as quickly as possible among would-be customers and other members of the trade. You want to stimulate a healthy volume of trade in as short a time as possible and you do not have the advantage of a shop window when your business is being conducted from home. Advertising in the widest sense and all other forms of publicity must be employed to launch your new venture.

At the beginning the publicity drive will have to be more intensive than when you have been trading for some time and you may find that waiting for customers to come and buy is disheartening. It is not enough to stock yourself up and tell a few friends what you are doing, you have got to get out and make yourself known. This takes a good bit of doing.

Your first goal is to obtain as much free advertising, or nearly free to be strictly honest, as you can. There are bound to be some fairly minor expenses involving the printing of cards and letter headings, but you are going to need these anyway. It is how you use them once you have them that really counts. A tycoon once said that he was spending twice as much money on advertising as necessary and the only thing stopping him cutting the expenditure in half was that he did not know which half to cut. Here is the problem: it is very easy to waste money on useless advertising and often hard to resist certain local appeals. But let us first look at basics.

Right from the start you want to create what advertising agents would call the correct image. Everything you do to publicise your business must be done with this in mind and it is the printed word that is generally more durable than a verbal introduction. The impact of letter headings and trade cards is considerable, so if they are cheap and badly laid out they leave behind them a sense of unease and doubts over trusting the trader they are meant to introduce. On the other hand, a smart well-presented introduction makes a favourable initial impression, tempting the recipient to explore further.

It is sensible to find a competent commercial artist to produce an attractive insignia and layout for the two basic essentials: a trade card and letter heading. Some kind of recognition symbol that will immediately identify you is a great aid to easy introduction. If it can create an association between either your name or your speciality, so much the better: a bow and arrow if your name is Archer, a holder of hatpins if you always have them to sell and buy. Once you are settled on a suitable simple thumbnail drawing for your 'trade mark', incorporate it as often as possible into all your advertising. Have a stock of photographic prints made so that they can be handed out whenever there is a chance to use it in any kind of announcement, in programmes or newspapers.

Trade cards are, if properly designed, by far your most important cheap form of advertising. Initially you want a lot of them so order five hundred. Once it is set up the cost of printing a few hundred more is negligible. Choose a tinted card or cover paper and a contrasting ink if you like, but don't allow them to become brash or garish. You do not need to have an expensive ivory board and engraved print. Your designer will assist you in making a suitable choice.

You should never miss an opportunity to drop cards on people who might be interested or could help by displaying them in places where they will be seen by possible customers. For instance you may be able to get friendly landlords of local hotels and public houses to display a card for you. In fact it is worthwhile considering a larger version of your card and having a small handbill printed, about 8 in by 7 in (20 cm by 18 cm), if you can find enough places to display them. Hotels, clubs and pubs will not charge for displaying a discreet notice if you are one of their occasional customers, but you may have to pay for displaying them on newsagents' boards and the like. If you live in an out-of-the-way place the inclusion of a sketch map is helpful.

By all means, too, rake in all your suitable friends to help. If you know them well, give them a supply of cards to spread around for you: the wider you can radiate the word the quicker you will build up your connection. It is also important to get your name around the trade. Whenever the opportunity arises distribute your cards to other dealers. Many of them keep trade cards in an index for reference purposes.

Up to now we have been examining the kind of publicity you can get for practically no cost at all. Never refuse free publicity but always be on your guard against publicity that looks as if it is free but in the end could cost you dear. This is usually in the form of trade directories or local guides to the district. Every now and again fly-by-night operators launch spurious directory companies and talk the unsuspecting into agreeing to have their name appear. There are, of course, a number of quite legitimate directory publishers, so check thoroughly to see exactly what you are committing yourself to.

You must also harden your heart against paying for useless local advertising, the kind which is designed to make money for the initiators rather than the advertiser. Most amateur dramatic society programmes, local carnival brochures, Chamber of Commerce guide books and parish magazines fall into this category. The advertising is designed to pay for their printing costs and the value to you, as the advertiser, is minimal at the best; look on them only as a charitable contribution if you must agree to participate. But examine every proposition critically, there are notable exceptions.

One of the cheapest and often most rewarding advertising mediums is the classified columns of the local papers, particularly the weeklies. In order to have the greatest impact you should advertise regularly over a sustained period. Many journals have reduced rates for long-term bookings but you may have to contract for three months or more to take advantage of them. The insertion can be very brief and only contain enough information to stimulate an enquiry. Once you have a personal contact, the rest is up to your powers of salesmanship. Advertisements like the following are the kind of thing that pulls:

Antique jewellery bought and sold. Best prices. Phone Hilary Wright on Buxton 1234

Antique clocks, large selection. I buy anything antique. Houses cleared. Jim Jones, 89 Hill Road, Hampton. Phone 1234

Postcards wanted. Albums, collections. Will travel to view. Large selection available. Phone for list Beckton 1234

Jean Fellows Antiques, Hole Manor, Broad Lane, Pinner. Brass, copper, clocks, porcelain, samplers. Open Tuesdays, Thursdays and weekends. Phone 1234

Some journals have a minimum rate for two or three lines or for a specified number of words. Enquire before composing your entry to gain maximum advantage. It is rather like composing a telegram in the days when we used to use them. In some papers, too, it may be advantageous to have an insertion under two or more classifications, such as 'For Sale' and 'Local Services'. This kind of publicity is parti-

51

cularly valuable when you are starting up, but you must monitor closely the response to paid advertising. If it doesn't pull in a worthwhile volume of enquiries, cancel it as soon as you can and try another approach.

If you become a specialist dealer, it may be worth trying some advertising in the antiques trade journals. Most of them have a classified or small insertions section and it is prudent to try them out with a modest announcement before graduating to a larger display advertisement over half a page or more. By the time you have specialised you will be aware of the particular journals read and used by the collectors and dealers in your speciality, but it is always important to be cautious before committing yourself to expensive advertising. The return has to be balanced against both the short-term sales and the long-term goodwill.

It is more than likely that there is a club or society which caters for enthusiasts in the speciality that interests you. Get to know about its activities. Many organisations, like the Musical Box Society as one example, publish an international list of members and hold regular meetings. Active participation in such societies is obviously of prime importance to anyone engaged in selling in a particular field.

Cigarette and trade card collectors also have national and international organisations. A monthly journal is produced by the leading company trading in cards and regular auctions and meetings, both national and local, for card collectors are held. If by chance you discover a specialist field which has no club, and you have a nucleus of interested collectors, you can always start a society.

Direct mail advertising, that is selling by sending out letters to known collectors who are interested, can also be a rewarding approach to any specialist market. Never miss an opportunity to make a note of names and addresses of collectors who ask for specific things, together with their requirements. You will eventually build up an invaluable and unique mailing list and, inspite of the cost of postage, can bring in a useful volume of business.

In any case it is always good tactics to keep in touch with regular customers and never miss an opportunity of putting your name before them. The technique in its simplest form is to circulate a duplicated list of the items which you currently have for sale. The description of each item should be as detailed as possible so that prospective buyers will have a complete mental picture of each piece on offer and will know what they are getting for their money.

As you will be circulating the list to prospective purchasers all over the country, and perhaps to addresses abroad as well, you should be prepared to send goods by post to your customers. The list must therefore also state details of your terms of business. Transactions should be on a 'cash with order' basis, even to customers you know well. You should also make it clear that money will be refunded in full on the safe return of goods if they prove to be unacceptable. Even extremely fragile articles can be sent through the post providing they are securely packed, preferably in a double carton and protected by some of the new lightweight plastic packing materials. It is often not appreciated that registered postal packages can be insured against breakage or loss in transit for a relatively low fee. I have sent ceramics all over the United Kingdom by post with remarkably few casualties.

Now let us turn from advertising in the strict sense to other forms of publicity, for they play an equally important part in the process of selling. One of the underexploited ways of selling antiques is holding coffee mornings or tea parties. As you know, this method of selling is widely employed for the promotion of jewellery, ladies underwear, plastic food containers, cosmetics and the like. There is no reason why you as an antique dealer should not take a leaf out of the large commercial corporation's book and do the same thing. If you are not sure how to go about this kind of selling, just join a Tupperware party and take notes.

The way may be made easier for you if there is one of the large number of antique clubs in your area. An approach to the secretary or chairman may be welcomed, particularly if you specialise in a popular subject and can offer a talk on your particular field. Of course clear with the organisation that they have no objection to your bringing along a collection of whatever you talk about and that some of them will be for sale. One group of regional clubs are sponsored and encouraged by *Antique Collecting*, the journal of the Antique Collectors Club, 5 Church St, Woodbridge, Suffolk.

Other organisations whose branch secretaries are always looking for speakers are Women's Institutes, Townswomen's Guilds, Round Table and Inner Wheel. These too will provide new points of contact, although you will not be able to offer goods for sale, so in all cases remember to make a liberal distribution of your trade cards.

In some areas there are well-established markets held every week and a market stall is always worth considering if there is a suitable venue within convenient distance. In London and some other big cities certain markets, like Portabello Road and Bermondsey, are devoted entirely to antiques, but many mixed markets are suitable places for an antiques stall, at least during the spring and summer months.

Increasingly, in provincial and county towns as well as the big centres, entrepreneurs are opening up antique markets. These are usually large premises which have been divided up into small booths or shop windows and rented out on a semi-permanent basis to a multiplicity of individual small dealers. The organiser is frequently the chief exhibitor and is usually prepared to look after and sell the goods displayed on a commission basis during the times that the various tenants are absent. Some of these undertakings are huge, with fifty or a hundred different traders participating, some are quite small, housing less than a dozen dealers' displays. Such concentrations attract the general public and give exposure to merchandise that would not otherwise be available. And remember, there is

54

no inter-dealer competition in antiques because everyone's stock is different and virtually unrepeatable.

Perhaps one of the most effortless methods of selling, particularly if you are in a tourist area, is to establish showcases in hotel foyers, holiday camps and the like. These are willingly tended by the reception staff who hold the keys and take the money on your behalf. Many hotels already have established showcases and many more will entertain installing them if you provide the cabinet, which should, if possible, be lit in order to attract maximum attention. A commission is paid to the hotel management for the provision of the showcase display and their assistance in completing sales. The rate of commission will, of course, have to be by negotiation and will depend to a great extent on the average value of the individual items offered for sale.

Another method of obtaining maximum exposure for part of your stock is to arrange with antique shopkeepers in the area you are covering during your buying trips to display some of your goods. This is much easier to arrange, again, if you specialise in something. Many dealers do not handle certain classes of antiques because either they do not know much about the subject and are not particularly interested or they just do not have sufficient capital to invest. It does not take much imagination to appreciate that an attractive collection of small articles in a self-contained display offered at no cost with a guaranteed profit on every sale is an attractive proposition.

I know one coin dealer who has trays of coins strategically placed in a dozen or so antique shops where the proprietors would not otherwise deal in coins. The displays have to be serviced and replenished on average about once every month or six weeks. A check is kept on sales by providing each shopkeeper with a duplicate list of the coins and the retail price. A self-adhesive price label is also placed below each coin in the display tray. As each coin is sold, the sale is recorded on the stock list with a note of the date sold. The space in the display tray is left vacant, showing the price label. When something like half the coins in a tray have been sold, a phone call brings the coin dealer to replenish the coins and collect his money — in this case less twenty per cent of the marked retail price. The stock list is corrected by striking out all items sold and adding details of the new coins and their retail price. The labels in the trays act as a double check.

Obviously similar schemes can be devised for all kinds of specialities, such as jewellery, hatpins, crested china, in fact anything that appeals to the specialist dealer and collector. A point not to be overlooked is that sales are likely to be stimulated considerably when a collection of similar articles is displayed, rather than just two or three examples.

As it is likely that you will be visiting and buying regularly from a number of antique shops, it stands to reason that you will be forging friendships with some of the owners and it is natural that a bond of mutual assistance will be built up. You, because you get around more than most of your shop-bound contacts will be able to look out on their behalf for things that they want to buy. Often you will be able to buy for them, once you get to know exactly what they require and the price they are prepared to pay. In other words the trade can easily become reciprocal and it is quite in order for you to charge a small percentage commission for the time and trouble you have expended in fetching and carrying.

The secret here, as with many other aspects of antique trading, is not to be too greedy. Lots of highly successful dealers make a handsome living in part out of turning over stock bought on the behalf of other dealers at a tiny margin of profit *and at a fast rate*. It is better, when you think about it, to buy and sell one twenty pound article a week at ten per cent mark-up than have a hundred pound article in stock for six months and make thirty per cent. In the first instance you have made £52.00 and in the second a profit of only £33.00.

Specialisation

Perhaps the first move to upgrade both your stock and your trade from just general dealing in small articles is to find a speciality. There are two distinct variations on specialisation in the antique trade: one is to confine your activities entirely to the buying and selling of a single kind of article, and the other is to concentrate on a variety of associated goods although not to the exclusion of general dealing.

In the first category you could, for instance, trade in nothing but antique glass in its various forms, or small articles made of wood (known as Treen), or fine porcelain. Some extremely successful dealers who have built up both a reputation and a large clientele of collectors have narrowed their field down even more by dealing only in wine glasses, Tunbridge ware or Worcester porcelain. Dealers in figurines may eventually concentrate on Chelsea or Bow and even dealers in furniture are likely to concentrate on, for instance, early oak, Regency mahogany and rosewood or even Art Nouveau and Art Deco, once they have built up a large enough outlet to provide a reasonable living from a restricted field.

More easily, and perhaps as a step towards more concentrated specialisation, the general dealer can start to restrict buying to a variety of specialities in which he or she has either a hobby interest, extensive knowledge, a continuous and untapped source of supply or a combination of all these elements. The one thing of paramount importance is to be able to provide sufficient volume of similar things that collectors in large enough numbers want to buy.

There is little point in becoming the leading authority on Victorian corset stays if there are only three collectors in the world, of which you and your next-door neighbour are two, unless you can achieve several things:

1 Discover a virtually limitless source of supply or hit on something that has been thrown away for centuries and

can be recovered.

2 Whip up an enthusiastic following who will want to collect items, possibly by starting a club and publicising it in the antiques press.

3 Ensure that examples at least of the commoner types of the article are available in large enough quantities for them to remain relatively cheap and so be available to collectors of modest means.

You may think that this is an impossibility, but it is not. The antique trade has thrived for centuries on finding things that most people want to discard, brightening them up and popularising them once more. Within the last decade there has been a huge following built up for collecting, to name but a few, different varieties of barbed wire; sections of railway and tramline rails; Nazi insignia; glass and earthenware bottles; and Railwayana.

Pot lids, beer mats, matchboxes, sheet music, autographs and letters, Chinese snuff bottles, as examples, have for years had a wide enough following to command specialist sales from time to time at leading London auction houses, while such things as Goss and other miniature armorial crested white porcelain momentoes have their own well-established collectors clubs and price guides.

To the best of my knowledge nobody has started to collect the individual packets of sugar which have for years been a feature of bar tables in Continental Europe and are slowly gaining favour in this country, but no doubt somebody will start taking the subject seriously in the end.

In Victorian and Edwardian times, when collecting was as popular as it is today and when specially engraved headed notepaper was commonplace the cult of collecting printed armorial crests became popular. Special albums were available, as are stamp albums today, for collectors to mount their collections, but the hobby died, perhaps because the supply dried up. Collections still turn up from time to time at auctions.

A specialist collection of converted gas lamps.

Some, in fact most, collectables start off by being cheap and easy to find only to become scarce and to price themselves beyond the pocket of all but the most dedicated collector. A few go on for ever like cigarette and trade cards, coins, postage stamps, postcards and buttons. There is always room for new dealers concentrating on the most popular collectables.

Some unlikely things like early wireless sets, gramophones and 78 rpm records, banknotes, foreign bonds, prewar Dinky toys and clockwork tinplate toys quickly became

59

much sought after and therefore expensive when they found a ready market. This is most likely due to the fact that they conjure up happy childhood memories or long-gone romantic fantasies of travel and wealth beyond practical possibility. In his *Price Guide to Collectable Antiques* (Chancery House Publishing Co, Woodbridge, Suffolk) James Macay lists 112 different types of collectables from aeronautica to wine labels and does not, as he admits in the foreword, even scratch the surface of the ephemera still to be turned into desirable and displayable collections.

You have only to walk round the average antiques fair to observe that a very large proportion of the stallholders have not bothered to analyse what they are selling and at best have only attempted a rudimentary grouping of a few examples of silver thimbles, vesta boxes, sugar tongs and teaspoons in one corner. A jar of a dozen or so hatpins here, a few coronation mugs and other bits of commemorative pottery there, surrounded by sundry bric-a-brac do not make much of a prestige show and most likely quickly cease to give much satisfaction to the owner as well.

Those stalls that contain a worthwhile volume of a few specialities stick out like beacons on a moonless night. It is a more than satisfying exercise to sit down and think about what you want to achieve and how you can attract favourable attention by giving some extra perspective to your display.

Of course it can be argued that many of the things that are collected these days are not antiques at all. While it is obvious that in due course of time they will eventually acquire an antique value, the purist may turn his nose up at collecting or dealing in contemporary or obsolescent junk. But people like to collect things and, because the prices of so much that is genuinely antique have sky-rocketed to heights beyond the average purse, they are bound to turn to other more modestly priced artifacts that will soon become desirable.

Anything that is interesting and has begun to acquire the

patina of age, has dropped from everyday use or is a part of social history is far more worthy of collecting than the grossly over-priced, spurious commemorative gold-plated medallions, decorated plates, model animals, miniature copies of classical vases and the like that depreciate in value faster than motor cars and will not be collectors' items for half a lifetime.

Anyone who decides to plough a furrow on virgin pasture will be faced with a load of problems. Whereas established fields already have a recognised scale of market values, with a new line of collectables you will have to pitch the prices at a realistic level. It is likely that there is no literature on the subject, so you will have to conduct a programme of research to establish a background for your chosen interest. Initially you will not be able to discover how many of the objects of your choice are to be found scattered round the country or gauge how many people are likely to take sufficient interest to want to start collecting. From a hobby point of view it may be of absorbing interest; on purely commercial lines it most likely will be a long-term project, or even a dead duck. But trading in antiques is not just a way of making money. Most people engaged in the trade are collectors too.

Once you have decided to specialise it is important to research the finer points of your speciality and be able, almost at a glance, to grade the various objects by age, type, method of manufacture, quality, aesthetic value, area of origin, kind of decoration, maker's trade marks, degree of perfection of reduction in value due to damage, rarity, desirability and so on.

It is these very analytical qualities that distinguish an authority from a run-of-the-mill dealer. As you acquire your reputation as an expert you will find that more and more people bring their things to you for an opinion and, inevitably, for sale and to buy. It is in knowing the scarce from the commonplace, the work of a leading craftsman from the factory-made, the degree of damage acceptable and the name of a willing buyer that makes specialisation a highly lucrative pursuit.

You will always find a disparity in price between different parts of the country, even between major and minor auction houses in the same city. You will also find that as many dealers will outrageously overprice as underprice objects of which they have only sketchy knowledge. The thrill is, of course, that around each corner there may be the find of a lifetime. If you have the specialist knowledge you will be able to recognise the find when it eventually turns up.

Transport

Transport is undoubtedly the greatest overhead that the antiques dealer who is trading from home has to face up to and in consequence it deserves careful examination and discussion.

It is of paramount importance that you are able to transport yourself and your stock to and from antiques fairs. You must also be mobile to pursue the never-ending search to replenish that stock. It is, of course, possible to accomplish this by public transport and Shanks Pony if you are dealing only in small bulk and reasonably high-value goods. But in order to be fully and efficiently mobile you need a motor vehicle that is reliable and, in these days of ever-escalating petrol prices, as economical as possible.

When you have really arrived in the antique trade it is generally acknowledged that you drive around in a Volvo Estate Car. The reason for this is that it has a huge carrying capacity and, most important, a very large rear door which will allow almost any piece of furniture free access. This is all very well if you are dealing mainly in antique furniture, but smaller and much more economical makes of car are more practical for the dealer in 'smalls'. To begin with, the smaller your car the easier it is to manoeuvre in built-up areas and to find parking spaces. This is important because you will spend a lot of time looking for convenient parking when visiting shops and markets. And while on the subject of parking, you can usually get away with a short stop on a single yellow line by claiming that you are loading or unloading. This is permitted if you are not causing an obstruction and you should be safe for twenty minutes.

It is not likely that you will want to carry very large loads of furniture and even if you do you can treble your carrying space by fitting a *professional* roofrack. The kind you want is a completely flat one made of tubular metal that covers the entire top of the vehicle. You often see them advertised in the antique trade press.

It is far easier to put a large piece of furniture on a roofrack than trying to manoeuvre it through the tailgate of a car. The lift onto a roofrack is not a difficult one but you should have an assistant: four hands are much surer than two. In the antique trade you will soon find that the complaint known as Dealer's Back is far too common. It is caused by lifting objects that are too heavy or getting your spine twisted by lifting things in and out of confined spaces where you cannot stand correctly to take the strain of an awkward load. When dealing with a heavy lump, try when you can to lighten the load by removing drawers etc.

It took me a long time to find out that a medium to small hatchback car fitted with a roofrack provides as much carrying capacity as you need and that it hardly ever rains when you have a load on top. It is nevertheless a wise precaution to carry a waterproof canvas or plastic cover, fitted with proper eyelets and ties to secure it just in case. Be mindful, though, of the fact that roofracks increase petrol consumption by over a penny a mile so take them off when they are not likely to be wanted. They are only secured by four thumbscrews and can easily be dismounted in a few moments.

When carrying furniture and other goods on a roofrack there are several rules that should be adhered to. First and foremost, see that the load is securely tied down. Do not use rope or string but carry with you a few lengths of up-holstery webbing — the 2 in (5 cm) wide hessian ribbon — which will not make chafe marks or rope burns, even over long distances. You should also learn how to tie slip knots that are trustworthy and easy to undo at the other end of the journey. And lastly, when you have a large load on top make allowances for wind resistance which can affect your steering and check that the load will neither slip sideways nor backwards and forwards.

If you consult the RAC or AA they will tell you the true cost of running a vehicle, currently 15 to 20 pence per mile, but this figure must be looked at carefully. It takes into consideration depreciation which, on a new car, can be £500 upwards in the first year, as well as petrol, licence, insurance, tyres, servicing and repairs. As most of you will be running a car anyway for convenience and pleasure some of these costs can be discounted or shared between pleasure and business.

As to insurance, you must check with your insurance company that your cover is adequate for business use. This may increase the premium, but it is essential to be properly insured. You should also consider insuring against theft from your car. This is normally available as an extra on your motor accident policy, but it is as well to shop around through a competent broker to get the best deal.

Most dealers soon learn how to pack a car to hold the maximum load. A hatchback vehicle without a high sill to lift things over or an estate car is almost an essential if you need to carry a good load inside. It is practice which makes perfect.

Breakables need secure padding against sudden jerks and must be prevented from rattling and rubbing together. Close packing together is the best safeguard. As suggested earlier, newspaper is the great standby as a buffer and all fragile items should be contained in cardboard boxes. Choose a combination of sizes that will fit exactly into the back of your car without sliding around.

Pieces of furniture and other polished items that are too big for boxes need protection against transit damage and, of supreme importance, protection against the effects of strong sunlight through glass windows. An hour, or even less, standing with full sunlight on a piece of polished furniture can wreak such havoc that the whole surface needs stripping and repolishing. Old blankets, on sale at any auction for a few pence, are the perfect solution to provide cover and the necessary stuffing to stop your load shifting while you are on the move. They are also useful for hiding things away from the eyes of potential thieves.

While on the subject of car security, always remember to lock all doors, including the tailgate, even if the vehicle is only out of your sight for a few moments. If you are in the habit of carrying valuable loads of small bulk consider having an alarm fitted.

When going out on buying trips it is sensible to sit down with a map for a few minutes and plan out your most economical route. You will be surprised at how many miles you can save and how many extra calls you can fit in with a little planning.

And, finally, beware of the customer who wants you to deliver for them, or anyone else for that matter who asks you to do them a favour that involves using your car − it is expensive in both time and money, and you are not running a delivery service. Always make that clear or take the cost into consideration when fixing the price of furniture which you most likely will have to deliver.

4   Cleaning and Renovation

It is obvious that anything in good and clean condition is far more desirable and is worth more money than when it is dirty and broken. But by their very nature, old things are inclined to become dilapidated and grimy, particularly when they have been cast aside for some time and only come to light when sent to auction as a result of house removal or clearance.

One of the recurring thrills of the antique trade is spotting the potential of something hidden at the bottom of a mixed lot of smalls in an old laundry basket or tin bath. These lots crop up at every country auction, but it is not only here that hidden treasure is to be discovered. It turns up at jumble sales, fairs, weekly markets, on junk stalls and in attics and farm barns, even in antique shops. The experienced dealer will always ask a shopkeeper if he has anything in the back store that might be of interest.

There are, of course, many professional restorers and renovators of all types of antiques and it is sensible to get to know where you can go for a competent restoration on furniture, ceramics and other articles, when you have unearthed something of great potential value or where the task of repair and reinstatement is beyond your own capabilities. In many cases, however, simple cleaning and refurbishing is relatively straightforward, requiring only time and a basic knowledge of the correct cleaning and mending techniques — and a little common sense.

The uninitiated are invariably scared of 'interfering' with old things 'in case they do more damage than good'. These fears are largely unfounded and in most cases dramatic improvements to the look and function of dirty and damaged artifacts can be achieved by judicious cleaning and polishing. But here a word of caution. Before you jump in with both feet carry out a careful examination of the article which is the candidate for your attention.

You must develop a practised eye for the really valuable prize hidden under layers of dirt and neglect. If in doubt get a skilled opinion before going to work on it. The staff of your local museum will be glad to offer assistance. The cost of skilled restoration is well worth the price when hundreds of pounds may be at stake. Don't be like the man who bought a pine-cased grandfather clock that had been painted brown. After he had started to strip it to his horror he found out too late that under the top coat of paint was Chinese lacquer decoration which he had also started to strip off. Suitable articles for non-professional restoration are, fortunately, in the majority and you should have no qualms over having a go.

The ideal for any antique is that it should look as if it has been lovingly maintained and protected from the day it left the manufacturer's workshop. Obviously it should bear the patina of age, have suffered some minor knocks and show a few signs of honest wear and tear. An over-restored article can be mistaken for a reproduction, so over-restoration is a mistake. You must have this firmly in your mind while working on any article; elimination of every last blemish is not necessarily perfection.

You must also decide in advance if the time you are going to spend on renovation is profitably spent. There is no point in spending a whole evening mending something when the result of your labour is only going to increase its value by a few pence. Better leave it in its present condition and let a customer have a bargain to take home and work on. They do not have to count the cost of the hours involved. Fortunately most restoration jobs result in a doubling or trebling of the value of the article.

The general dealer should be equipped to take on the cleaning and renovation of almost anything that may pass through his or her hands. These articles will mainly fall into the following general categories:

Wood	Metals
Ceramics	Bone
Textiles	Glass
Stone	Paintings

Different cleaning and mending materials are needed for each, but a relatively small outlay will equip the average dealer to undertake a wide variety of tasks. The following is no more than a guide to basic principles. There are several specialist books on the market dealing in greater detail with the various techniques.

Wood

Most antique wood has been polished at some time by one of the two basic methods that have been traditionally employed: (a) wax polishing and (b) varnish or French polishing.

The most easily undertaken renovation is simple cleaning down and rewaxing. For cleaning off the accumulation of dust, grime and old polish use fine to medium wirewool and white spirit (turpentine substitute) as a solvent and lubricant. Scour the surface of the article taking care to rub in the direction of the grain, not across it if this can be avoided. If it can't, watch out that you don't make deep scratches. You can substitute a rag for the wirewool, but it will need more rubbing and take longer. Turps substitute will remove all old dirt-impregnated wax polish but will not attack varnish polish or French polish. Very often the mere removal of this surface dirt etc followed by a new coat of good quality wax polish will be all the renovation required.

If you find that the old varnish or French polish is crazed or has ceased to be translucent, has become yellowed and the grain of the wood is partly obscured, it is time to remove this polish also by employing an efficient paint stripper. Nitromors is the best which is universally available from paint and DIY shops.

Once you have removed the last speck of old polish and produced a clean, flat surface, repolish it with a solid antique-quality wax polish. There are a number on the market, but it is worth while getting a supply of Gedges No.7 (see the directory at the back). French polishing is not difficult with the newer materials on the market; get a pack of Furniglas and experiment.

If the colour has faded badly, brighten it up before polishing with one of the non-varnish stains. The Coloron range is excellent. For concealing and rectifying odd scratches and scrapes, keep a complete range of all the colours of shoe polishes. These coloured waxes are the standby for instant repairs employed by all antique dealers. For minor repairs to veneers which have become detached or loose and for other small sticking jobs, use one of the all-purpose quick-drying acrylic or polystyrene adhesives in tubes, like Uhu and Gloy Polystyrene, which are available from stationers shops. While the glue is drying hold the joint firmly in place with Sellotape.

For bigger repairs use one of the white plastic wood glues, such as Evostick Resin W or Borden, which come in plastic squeeze bottles and are easy to use but take longer to harden. Successful glueing is easy if you adhere strictly to three rules. (1) Make sure that both surfaces to be glued are absolutely clean and free from all traces of old glue. (2) Make sure that both surfaces come into close contact all over the surface to be joined — you cannot glue together fresh air. (3) After glueing ensure that the two elements are firmly clamped together and cannot move for at least twelve hours. Avoid using screws and nails, they make unsatisfactory joints and are the devil to remove and conceal when a proper glued repair is being made.

One of the biggest deterrents to a sale is evidence of

woodworm. Although irrational, the objection to the signs of woodworm has to be countered. The easiest remedy is to fill the exit holes with wax polish, or better still use the appropriate shade of one of the patent woodfillers, such as Brummer. In really old furniture it is very doubtful that any active woodworm survives. It can be reintroduced by fitting new plywood backs to chests of drawers or replacing such parts as drawer bottoms, but a thorough brushing over with a woodworm killer gives permanent protection against reinfestation if active insects are by chance present.

Ceramics

Normally a thorough wash in warm water containing some washing-up liquid will remove most of the grime, but be careful not to break or chip fragile articles; protect them by putting a foam plastic sheet in the bottom of the sink if you have several articles to cleanse.

Badly-stained teapots and cups can sometimes be freed from the accumulation of tannin etc by overnight soaking in household bleach, or better still in one of the proprietary stain removers such as Chempro T or Stainfree from Boots or other larger chemists. Long-standing cracks get contaminated with dirt and stains and bleaching may also reduce or remove the discolouration.

Broken and chipped pieces can be repaired with either Epoxy resin adhesives like Araldite or the new Cyanoacrylic adhesives (Locktite). Use as little glue as possible applied to both surfaces, which must be absolutely free of grease and dust. After joining hold the parts together with strips of adhesive tape (paper is best) and carefully wipe away all excess glue before it dries.

Missing areas, if they are fairly small, can be repaired with a special ceramic putty, such as Sylmasta (from art shops) or alternatively make your own by mixing Araldite with a suitable white filler, such as Kaolin or Titanium

Oxide, until it forms a stiff paste. This can be moulded and, when dry, rubbed and filed down to conform with the rest of the article. If required any colouring can be done with acrylic paints and given a final glaze with one of the special materials available from art and craft shops, such as Chintex.

Old repairs, badly executed and probably discoloured because animal glues were used, can be broken by soaking them in hot water or heating in a medium oven. Riveted repairs are not usually worth taking apart unless the piece is of exceptional value. For some reason customers will accept riveted repairs as being a proof of age.

Textiles

Here common sense has to be used. Many things, such as lace and embroidery, may have become very fragile by exposure to light, wear and tear and constant laundering. Often the material may be yellow with age and stained. Before attempting any treatment such fragile fabrics must be supported by tacking them to nylon net, such as net curtaining.

Very often no more than several successive soakings in distilled or softened water will remove accumulated dirt. Avoid scrubbing or violent agitation: even light rubbing must be carried out with great care when handling old materials. If stains persist, try spirit soap (from chemists) at 1 oz (28 g) to a pint of water. Peroxide of hydrogen is the bleach used by the trade, but beware of causing the fabric to disintegrate.

With coloured or dyed materials you must test *each colour* for fastness before proceeding with cleaning. Again, use spirit soap to clean and only rock the article backwards and forwards with it suitably spread out in a bath or basin.

Non-fast colours and some persistent stains can be cleaned with dry cleaning fluids, such as Carbon Tetrachloride. This fluid is non-flammable but the fumes are obnoxious so only use it outside or in a well-ventilated room. It can be used for both allover and spot treatment.

Repairs, if you are handy with a needle, should be carried out with old threads rather than modern ones where possible. If you have to use new cottons, bleach them down to match by soaking in a household bleach before use. Always mend cotton material with cotton thread, linen with linen and silk with silk.

Stone

There is a vast range of various stones used for the manufacture of all kinds of artifacts which are liable to turn up in the antique trade. Some are soft and easily damaged like soapstone and alabaster, some extremely hard like granite and slate.

As a general rule washing with warm soapy water followed by drying and burnishing with a chamois leather will remove surface dirt and grease. A. Bell & Co of Kingsthorpe, Northampton NN2 6LT supply direct a range of stone cleaning, bleaching and polishing materials suitable for a wide range of different stones from marble to York stone. After thorough washing and cleaning, most stonework for interior display looks better if it is polished. First burnish surfaces with a dry washleather then apply a coating of microcrystalline wax polish.

Breaks and chips can be repaired with Epoxy Resin adhesives which, if required, can be coloured with pigments (powder paints) and missing pieces restored with a mastic made by adding a filler to the adhesive or using a suitably coloured mix of Sylmasta, as with ceramics.

Metals

In some cases ordinary household polishing materials,

such as Brasso or Duraglit, will be sufficient for cleaning brass, copper or other non-ferrous metal articles. For silver and precious metals Goddards Foam Cleaner is by far the best and most durable cleaner. If, however, as is often the case, tarnish is heavy and long periods of neglect have resulted in the article turning black, green or a combination of both, stronger measures are called for. An effective traditional treatment is to scour the surfaces with half a lemon liberally sprinkled with cooking salt, alternatively use a hot bath made up with a pint of boiling water, a cup of vinegar and a heaped teaspoon of salt. The next most easy method is a good non-caustic paint stripper. This should be applied with a brush, left for a few minutes to do its work and then washed off.

If you have a revolving buffing wheel you can buy special blocks of buffing compound containing oxalic acid which will polish up brass and copper in a very few minutes. A solution of oxalic acid and salt is also effective and rapid. Watch and clock repairers use a material called Horolene which is made up into a bath and the article is totally immersed in it for a period. This will remove even the most persistent tarnish. You can buy it from clockmakers' sundriesmen.

After cleaning and burnishing, bright surfaces can be preserved from further oxidation by polishing with a good-quality wax polish. This will prolong the shine for months before cleaning is required again.

Iron and steel call for rather different tactics as rust is likely to be encountered. After a thorough brushing-over with a wire brush to remove all loose scale and oxidation, a twenty-four-hour soak in paraffin oil will clean back to sound metal. After thoroughly drying off an application of Jenolite Jelly Rust Remover and Preventer will deposit a layer of iron phosphate which will inhibit any further rusting. A final traditional polish to black iron can be imparted with the modern equivalent of blacklead, Zeabrite, manufactured by Rickett and Coleman, Hull. Alternatively a coat

73

of matt finish black paint can be applied, but I always prefer a blacklead or bright finish.

Ivory, Bone and Horn

Before the introduction of plastics a huge variety of articles, from snuff boxes to combs and handles, was manufactured from various types of bone and horn. Today many of them are highly collectable and command quite high prices on the antique market.

Most discoloured bone articles can be bleached and cleaned by the application of a stiff paste made of Kaolin (china clay) mixed with Hydrogen Peroxide. Let the paste dry on the article and then gently brush it off with a soft brush. Many types of bone and horn are sensitive to prolonged wetting, so if they are washed in soapy water they should be dried off immediately.

Repairs can be undertaken with Epoxy Resin or PVA adhesives and a final polish given with microcrystalline wax or almond oil.

Glass

Nearly all glass is brittle and therefore easily broken. The better the quality of crystal, the more fragile it becomes, so great care has to be taken when cleaning old and valuable glass.

Normally a wash in warm water containing a little detergent is sufficient followed by a rinse in water with a proportion of ammonia added to make the glass sparkle. Narrow-necked vessels like decanters and bottles often present a problem of access. Wire-handled bottle brushes do some good, but often will not dislodge the last remnants of tenacious residues. Spirits of salts (Hydrochloric Acid) will remove any lime and hard water deposits and

74

many other stains. As an alternative try an overnight soak with one of the denture cleaners, such as Steradent, or swilling a mixture of sand and water around inside the vessel, but beware of scratching. If stains still persist or you find that the interior remains milky, this may be caused by slight etching and you will have to consult a glass expert to get it removed.

Minor chips to rims and lips of vases and other glass articles can often be rubbed down with fine carborundum stone, the sort used for sharpening chisels. A professional glassworker will turn down chipped lips and remove other flaws on a glass cutting wheel.

New adhesives specially made to repair glass have become widely available through hardware shops under the trade name of Locktite Glass Bond. This glue uses the ultraviolet light present in daylight to harden it. In bright sunlight it dries in less than ten seconds, in subdued light it may take two minutes or more and it will not dry in artificial light containing no ultraviolet.

Always make sure that the surfaces to be joined with glue are absolutely free from any grease or dirt by washing off with methylated spirit, or some other solvent. Apply the adhesive sparingly and wipe away any glue that exudes with a swab moistened with solvent. These new adhesives make an invisible joint as the refractive index is adjusted to be the same as the most common types of glass.

Paintings

It is normal practice for oil paintings to be protected shortly after completion with a coat of varnish and in due course of time this varnish yellows, collects dust, smoke and tobacco stains. In consequence the painting becomes darker and darker until most of the detail and the original brightness of the colours fade behind the murk.

Most oil paintings are executed on canvas stretched on a

wooden frame or on wooden panels, although you may find them painted on metal and man-made boards. Slack canvases can usually be tightened up by tapping the wedges at each corner of the frame a bit further in.

Picture cleaning is an expert undertaking and it is easy for the untrained amateur to do great damage to a painting, so do not practise on anything that might be very valuable. There is no reason, on the other hand, why you should not have a go at works of art purchased for a few pounds. Most important is to take your time and not go too far, otherwise you will find that you have wiped off all the rigging on the ship that has been subjected to your ministrations.

Cleaning away the old varnish can be done with one of the specially formulated varnish removers made by the leading artists' material manufacturers and sold in art shops. The technique is to treat a small area, applying the fluid on a clean wad of cotton wool, and to stop the operation the second any trace of colour − that is the paint − starts to show on the wad.

When dealing with paintings of little or no artistic merit, one method of cleaning that can be most effective is to wash over the surface with a household cleaner, such as Flash, but test it out on a corner first to see what the result is likely to be. Fortunately you can't lose money on these as new canvases are expensive and amateur artists will be glad to buy old ones to paint over. More serious deterioration, such as cracking, flaking and tears, is best left to the professional restorer if the finished result is likely to yield a profit. Watercolours and pastels are extremely dangerous to touch without expert knowledge.

Discoloured prints and engravings can be treated to remove stains and spots, known as foxing. The treatment is to support the sheet of paper on a glass sheet and soak it in distilled or softened water contained in a shallow tray. The glass supporting sheet is needed because as soon as it is wet the print will lose its strength, although it will not disintegrate.

In many cases stains will soak out in water alone if it is changed several times, but foxing will not yield to this treatment. Where discolouration persists use a mild bleaching agent; the most easily obtained is Chloramine T. You can chance your arm with a weak solution of Milton. Spot treatment can be given to particularly difficult areas of foxing with a watercolour brush if overall soaking does not work: use the same chemicals in stronger solutions. Always watch out for prints signed by the artist, the signature may not be permanent in the same way as the printing ink of the print. Dry the print between sheets of blotting paper while retaining the sheet of glass as support. In order to prevent distortion use a wad of newspapers on top of the blotting paper and books as a weight until the print is reasonably dry.

5 The Business End

The attitude of the vast majority of small business people to account keeping, form filling and dealing with bureaucracy is to do as little as possible, avoid contact where possible and generally keep their heads down. This is indeed a good policy, providing that the minimum of essential record-keeping is undertaken and *regularly kept up-to-date*. You need to avoid paying as much tax as you can so keep the simplest records which tell you exactly what you want to know and waste as little of your time as possible.

The one thing that you should under no circumstances do is to carry on merrily trading for two or three years hoping that the Inland Revenue will not catch up with you — they will. So from the very start of your business it is common sense to comply with the law, tell the taxman what you are doing and, above all, consult an accountant. His is the best advice you can buy and he will save his fee time and time again in avoiding the unnecessary payment of tax by claiming the full entitlement of relief on your behalf. Incidentally, married women can earn a considerable income without any liability to pay income tax.

But let us start at the beginning and look first at the simple records that are essential to the small trader who wants to know where he or she stands as far as profit and loss is concerned.

Book-keeping
You need no special talent for keeping records or, if you prefer to call them so, books. All you have to do is to

discipline yourself to make a note of every transaction. Never try to rely on your memory for longer than is absolutely necessary. Leaving things for days or months only results in your having to cook up some sort of half-remembered account which is unsatisfactory for everyone, most of all you.

The basic record book that you need is, for want of a better description, a stock book. In this you enter every item you buy, give it a reference number, record the date of purchase and the price paid. This applies to things of your own that you put into your stock when you first start, although date and price will have to be notional. When you sell anything, you record the date of sale and the price obtained. This is simplified by retaining the price tag from the article which bears the reference number and the other details. At an appropriate time a simple subtraction sum will give you the gross profit.

This kind of record shows you at a glance the things that sell quickly and those that stick. From time to time you may want to consolidate your stock records by bringing forward in the book those items that have remained unsold for too long, say at the end of each financial year. This will remind you that you have to do something about them — reduce the price or put them in auction perhaps — for dead stock is money lying idle which should be working for you.

As an additional check on the health of your business and also to prevent business money getting muddled up with private money, from the start it is sensible to open a separate bank account. Your monthly bank statement will show you how you stand from the cashflow point of view. You should ask the bank for both chequebook and paying-in book with counterfoils (not just a couple of pages at the front to record details of each transaction) and if necessary go to another bank if your present one can't oblige.

When using cheques always fill in the counterfoil first, then you won't forget to do it and you will get the details straight before you write the cheque. By doing this you will know in a year's time where the money went and where it came from without any heart-searching or memory-dredging. Whenever you want to know exactly where your business stands all you have to do is total up the purchase price column of those items still unsold in your stock book and add this figure to the balance on your bank statement. (I assume that you are unlikely to have any unpaid bills as antique dealing is a cash trade.) This total is the capital invested in the business.

For convenience sake, for example at antiques fairs, when you will not want to be lumbered with a stock book, keep a running record during the day of both sales and purchases in a notebook. These can be transferred to your stock book at a convenient time after the fair.

The one important thing that your stock book will not record is your out-of-pocket expenses for such things as petrol, hiring stands, meals out and other sundry overheads. In order to discover what your real profit is — your net profit — you must also keep an accurate record of these expenses in another book. It is very easy to forget such things as telephone calls, tips at auction rooms for portering and bidding on your behalf, incidental purchases of polish and other renovating sundries. It is always helpful to pay for these by cheque whenever possible and the sum is large enough to warrant it. But remember that bank charges can mount up considerably, so you should try to keep enough money in your current account to obtain your banking free. (It is not free, in fact, as the bank is using the money for lending but it is the best deal you can get for the convenience obtained.)

For a small business the services of an accountant should not cost you very much and the sooner you consult one the better. He will assist you with how to keep records if you are unsure of what to do and with other tasks like preparing a balance sheet and a tax return.

If you decide to carry on a business in any name other than your own or if you have a partner and are not trading under both your names in full you are bound by law to register the business name you are using within fourteen days of commencement of trading. This also applies to married women trading under their maiden name. The Registrar of Business Names, Pembroke House, 40-56 City Road, London EC1 (for Scotland 102 George St, Edinburgh) is the address to which you must write. You must also let him know if you cease trading or change the nature or name of your business. When you have registered you have to show the business name on letterheads and other literature as well as the full names of all owners of the business.

As soon as you start trading you should inform the local Inspector of Taxes and at the end of the first year's trading (which in fact can be extended to more than a year) you will have to present a properly drawn up balance sheet showing profit or loss. This is where the services of an accountant are valuable, but it is prudent to do as much as possible yourself to prepare a clear statement of your business affairs before you call him in. The more you do the less the accountant has to do and this will reduce his bill — it is his time that you will be paying for, as well as his expertise.

As you can deduct all kinds of expenses from the money you have made during the year, the book in which you kept a note of those expenses is important to your accountant. In addition he will find other costs incurred in the running of the business that you are entitled to claim and which you may have overlooked, like lighting and heating, that part of your home used for business purposes etc. The concessions for tax purposes change from year to year and it is the job of accountants to make sure that their clients take full advantage of them.

Help for Small Businesses
An extremely useful and virtually free service available to anyone contemplating starting a small business, or already

running one, is the Small Firms Service run by the Department of Industry. This information and counselling organisation will advise you on every aspect of small business from finance to export. It can put you in touch with libraries, chambers of commerce and other bodies who can help you with problems. It also runs a counselling service of experienced businessmen who can offer impartial advice and guidance in strict confidence. All you have to do to get into contact with them is dial 100 on the telephone and ask for Freefone 2444 which will put you in touch with your nearest centre. If they cannot answer your query on the spot or put you in touch with the right source of help, they will invite you to meet a counsellor at their local office. This information service is free. For counselling after one free exploratory session a modest charge is made for the second and subsequent sessions.

National Insurance

All self-employed people are required to pay a National Insurance contribution if and when they earn over a certain amount which goes up at Budget time most years. You need to inform your nearest Social Security office and apply for exemption while your earnings are below the minimum amount. When you become liable to pay you can either buy stamps from a Post Office or, better still, pay a lump sum at the time your accountant prepares your annual accounts. He will attend to these details if you ask him to do so. Government leaflet NI 41 will give you up-to-date information and other details.

Regulations and exceptions relating to married women are somewhat complex, but an interview with the local Social Security office will clarify individual situations. In all events you will have to pay a contribution with Schedule D income tax if you earn above the minimum limit (£2250.00 in late 1981). You can employ a casual helper without any liability to pay a National Insurance contribution if their total annual earnings are below about £1000.

It is not worth worrying about these regulations; your accountant will sort it all out for you, and anyway you can expect to have a clear run without the tax authorities worrying about you for at least two years. But the sensible thing is to be prepared when they do take an interest by keeping proper records from the start.

As your business expands you may feel inclined to join one of the Antique Trade Associations. The most important is The British Antique Dealers Association, 20 Rutland Gate, London SW7 1BD (phone 01-589 4128). The Association is highly prestigious, influential and demands high standards from its members. Joining is beyond the ambitions of all but a handful of dealers from home. (I only know of one, who buys and sells Worcester porcelain.) The other nationwide association is the London and Provincial Antique Dealers Association, 112 Brompton Road, London SW3 1JJ (phone 01-584 7911) whose entry requirements are more modest. Once you begin to participate in larger fairs and exhibitions membership is a distinct advantage as reduced rates are available to LAPADA members for stands, and also auction charges.

VAT

When and if your business expands to such a size that you are turning over a substantial figure (in late 1981 this was £15,000 per year or £5,000 in any one quarter) you become liable to Value Added Tax regulations. In other words you become an unpaid tax collector and are lumbered with a considerable volume of somewhat complicated paper work. By far the best thing to do is to split your business up and give part of it away to one of your children, an interested friend or someone else you can work with. You must both conduct separate businesses but you can have the same address and help each other.

In the antique trade there are two separate systems of VAT in operation. The first is the normal and compulsory addition of fifteen per cent to the selling price of each article. The second is a special optional scheme by which the tax is levied only on the difference between the purchase price and the selling price, ie the gross profit. For anyone selling articles of high value, indeed for anyone who has a liability to operate a VAT scheme, the Antiques Special Scheme (the second system) is worth operating even though it involves keeping a thirteen-column ledger and recording the identity of both the customer and the person from whom the article was bought.

Whether or not to get involved in VAT depends on your ambitions to expand your business. Most dealers in smalls appear to prefer to restrict their trading to a level which exempts them from participation. This means that when they buy from a VAT-registered source they cannot reclaim the VAT element from these purchases. There is, of course, no element of VAT when you buy from a private individual or from another non-registered dealer.

You may find it necessary from time to time to issue invoices for which you will require an invoice book in duplicate or triplicate. Indeed if you are operating a VAT scheme invoicing of sales is required. Some customers will ask you for an invoice as proof of the sale and you are required by law to provide one if requested. Some dealers invoice all sales for accounting purposes, but the vast majority of smalls dealers only issue invoices when asked to do so. It looks more businesslike if your invoice has a printed heading. One solution is to use your letter headings for invoicing, another is to use the small self-adhesive stickers that can be purchased for a few pounds a thousand, supplied by mail order and from most large stationers and use a standard invoice book.

You may also be asked, particularly by customers from overseas, to provide written authentication of an article and certify that it is over a hundred years old. Be very cautious in these cases and do not issue any statements of a doubtful nature as they can bounce back on you. Far better to say that you cannot be sure of the age if you are in doubt and just write a description of the article. Remember you can be liable under the Trades Descriptions Act if you falsely describe any article.

Overseas customers taking goods out of Britain are entitled to reclaim any VAT paid and in order to do this need special invoices for the Customs and Excise. Even if you are not operating VAT you may be asked by Continental buyers for invoices recording less money than in fact has been paid for goods. This is so that they can try to defraud their own customs authorities. The best advice is to refuse, they will still buy and being a party to this kind of deception leaves a nasty taste in the mouth.

Suing for Debt
Mention has previously been made to the fact that antique dealing is essentially a cash trade. It is far better to keep it so. Do not allow anyone to talk you into giving credit in any form. Cash on the nail always should be your rule; it safeguards you and does not lead to broken friendships. This also applies to goods on approval. Ask the person to pay before 'Taking it to show to my friend'. Tell them that you will refund their money if it is not suitable and returned within a specified time − not too long a time. This only applies to casual customers, of course, not to other dealers with whom you have special arrangements to display your wares.

Should you ever find yourself in the unfortunate position of being owed money by someone who will not pay, nowadays you do not have to face the expense of employing a solicitor and maybe ending up by throwing good money after bad. For some time there has been a simplified procedure whereby you can make application direct to the

Small Claims section of any County Court. You do not need the assistance of a solicitor, the procedures are designed to be straightforward and easy for the ordinary citizen to use.

The easiest way to to find out what to do is to call at your local Citizens' Advice Bureau or, if you know where it is, direct to the County Court. To start proceedings you ask for a *Request Form* from the Clerk of the Court's office and fill in details of the name and address of the person you are suing, your claim and your own address etc. You will have to pay a modest court fee, depending on the size of your claim, and the only other cost is £3 for serving the summons. When the claim is for a fixed sum there is no necessity for you to appear in court unless the claim is disputed. In this case a preliminary hearing is called and with any luck the registrar will settle the dispute on the spot without the necessity of a court appearance.

If you win you can apply for payment of your expenses, if you lose you will have to pay your opponent's court fees, travelling expenses and loss of earnings during the appearance. That is all. In practice nearly all non-payers will pay up at the first sign of a summons, as these days County Court debt cases are invariably picked up by the credit agencies and affect adversely future applications on the part of the person failing to pay their debts for hire purchase and other forms of credit.

We have discussed briefly the advantages of maintaining a separate bank account for your business, but banks have uses other than just minding your money. They are sources of capital. Indeed, in most cases, when you need to borrow money to buy extra stock, a more suitable car, or for any other expansion scheme, your bank manager is most likely the best and cheapest source for relatively small borrowing.

Banks make most of their profits by lending money and you need have no hesitation in approaching your bank manager when you need finance. He is able to lend sums up to about £1000 immediately on his own authority. You will naturally have to convince him that your reason for borrowing is a sound one and that you will be able to pay the bank back, with interest, within a specified time. But don't just go and ask for an overdraft on your current account because this may not be what you want and may cost more in interest payments than other kinds of bank loans. Ask your bank manager for his advice: he will be glad to assist you in any way he can, that is what he is there to do.

Planning Laws

When a business is being conducted from a private house care must be taken not to contravene the Planning Regulations. The law involved is the Town and Country Planning Act of 1971 which says that if any *material* change in the use of a building is involved, planning permission is required. The difficulty is that every Local Authority tends to put a different interpretation on *material change*.

From a practical point of view, the last thing on Earth that you should do is to ask your local council if you can conduct a business from your home. All you will succeed in doing is to alert some bureaucrat to your activities and give him an opportunity to oppose them. In fairness his position is a difficult one, for if he says there is no objection and at some time in the future someone does object, and then you say that the man from the council said it was all in order, the planning officer involved is in trouble. The sensible thing to do, therefore, is to keep your head down and do nothing to draw unwanted official attention to your activities.

The use of part of a private house for part-time and occasional business activities does not require planning permission as it involves no *substantial* change of use, but must depend on the degree of use before anyone can say that a *material* change of use has taken place. You are only likely to run into trouble if you start turning a large part of your house over to the storage and sale of antiques, involving a variety of people calling at your door, loading and unloading vehicles in such a way as to cause obstructions and generally annoying some or all of your neighbours. Indeed any complaint from a neighbour is likely to bring a man from the council round to make enquiries.

Be cautious, therefore, about erecting any kind of advertising sign outside your house saying, for instance, ANTIQUES, no matter how discreet you think it may be. (There are laws about signs too.) On the other hand there can be no objection to a nameboard saying you live there, if it is not too large.

It will be quite acceptable to apply for an entry in the Yellow Page phone directory announcing that you are dealing in antiques and for your private address to be used on business letterheads, advertisements in the press and shop windows etc providing these do not invite customers to call at the house, rather to write or phone. Beyond this you must do nothing that could be construed as any kind of *development* like, as an example, using your garage as a sort of shop or your front window to display things.

Occupants of council houses have to be doubly careful as most local housing authorities specifically ban the carrying on of any kind of business from council property intended for private living accommodation.

Planning permission for change of use of all or part of a private residence can, of course, be applied for and granted, provided that objections, if any, can be overcome. However, a change of use will inevitably lead to an increase in rates which are very much higher on commercial premises. But do not fret over this aspect: the worst that can happen is that in the first instance the council will tell you to cease business activity from a private address.

All this may make starting up a business on your own appear a formidable task, but it is not. Providing that you do not start out being totally dependent financially on the success of your enterprise, you can ease yourself into it as slowly as you like. You can start off with as little as ten pounds capital and spend only a few days a month on selling your wares. You can start out by developing a hobby and extending it to buy and sell only those things that interest you. You can start by making a study of some aspect of research on a subject that has taken your fancy. You can take a stall on a market for two or three pounds and sell your household bric-a-brac. Many successful dealers have started from such humble beginnings.

On the other hand, if you do want to start a full-time career in antique dealing, make sure that your initial capital is sufficient to support you for at least the first year, for it takes time to get known and to build up a reputation. If you are lucky enough to find someone who wants a partner or a paid assistant, take the job or the partnership for as long as it takes you to learn the basics. It may be frustrating, but someone else is in part financing your education. Far better to start off cautiously, learn thoroughly and acquire confidence than to jump in with both feet only to find that you are unable to get out again as quickly as you got in.

Good luck to you, and successful trading.

6   Case Histories

Frances Males

Frances started selling antiques ten years ago when her husband, who was an industrial chemist, was made redundant. At the time she had two grown-up children, both at college, and a young daughter who was five years old, so she had to find an income which could be earned largely from home while she was performing her household duties at the same time as running a business.

Before marriage she had held down a job in the art studio of an advertising agency and had had formal art training so felt confident that she could distinguish between good and bad in both art and design. She had always had an eye for old things, and indeed still had a collection of things that she had bought or been given as a child. She had haunted jumble sales and realises, on looking back, that she has always possessed an ability for sorting out the wheat from the chaff at bric-a-brac sales. When young, Frances loved to collect little pieces of porcelain and china that were covered with forget-me-nots and other flowers, like Coalport posies and houses. She also loved drawing and decorating things, a talent which she finds extremely lucrative today.

Both she and her husband decided that antiques were the best thing to go into. She could have started a restaurant as she is a well above average cook, but this would have meant her husband finding some other interest as he did not like the idea of becoming a restaurateur, and so they decided to try their hands at antiques. Husband David was a competent woodworker who could combine his talent with a part-time job which he had managed to find. She could put her art training to work on restoring ceramics.

When buying bits and pieces she had always wanted to make them look perfect but she was entirely self-taught and felt that she could not afford the price of a course which would have cost a couple of hundred pounds. The dilemma was solved by borrowing the notes from a friend who had recently been to classes and supplementing these with books from the local library. Once she got down to it, Frances found that she had a natural sympathy with the techniques of ceramic repairs and restoration, and an unerring instinct for spotting suitable articles to show a profit when restored.

She turned the front room into a 'shop', but found that very few people came in, in spite of the fact that the windows of her Georgian house were clearly visible from the street, so she started going to fairs at the weekends. The first fair that she did was a charity fund-raising effort held in an open stable. She says that she did everything wrong, including packing her stock in packing cases too heavy to lift by herself and arriving late after everyone else had set up their stands. This, however, turned out to be an unexpected piece of good luck as everyone gathered round while she unpacked and as a result she sold a large part of her stock and took a lot of money. This encouraged her to concentrate on fairs and find out how many she could get into over a fairly wide area.

Frances says that she quickly found out what a cut-throat world antique fairs are. She recalls a pair of Art Nouveau candlesticks which she had grossly underpriced. They were snapped up by another dealer as soon as they were exhibited, and promptly sold again at a greatly increased price to a runner. They later changed hands again to appear on yet another stall — all within the space of less than an hour.

It did not take long for Frances to decide that there were far too many dealers at fairs concentrating on fine porcelain, jewellery and small silver items. She wanted her stall to look different and to this end she started to buy metal items, particularly old kitchen equipment. In his spare time her husband repaired and polished them for her and now specialises in the renovation of metal goods of all kinds which are a feature of her extremely attractive stalls.

She also found that she could lose a lot of money through ignorance of items that passed through her hands, particularly silver and jewellery, so now keeps a comprehensive library of reference books and is always ready to seek expert advice. Increasingly she buys better pieces when she can to upgrade her stock, but still complains that lack of capital is the most frustrating brake on the expansion of her business.

For a time she feels that her business stood still, which should not have been allowed to happen, and now believes that to succeed anyone must go on upgrading the quality of their stock and knowledge of what they are handling. She points to people in the trade who started before she did and still do not really know what they are doing, but says that she thanks God for them because they provide a constant source of bargains!

Frances says that she has also found that it is who you know as much as what you know that matters. You must have sure sources of supply and cultivate them. This takes time and you must learn who you can trust and, just as important, have them feel that they can trust you. You must also know what you want to buy. It is also important to have the locals calling on you. Some come regularly and act as agents — old people with time on their hands welcome the chance of earning a bit of extra money and some of them really need it so they should always be given a square deal.

Frances says that it has taken years to work up a clientele that visits her regularly to buy certain specific things. Some come from the other end of the country once or twice a year and she keeps back the things they want in order to ensure that they keep on coming. Because her house is near a major port linking Britain with the Continent, there has been a larger than usual number of European dealers calling, most of them regular visitors on buying trips. Unfortunately this trade is right down at present, due to the strength of the Pound and recession in the European trade, but a few stalwarts still pay regular calls. Frances says all foreign dealers have their idiosyncrasies; she has one Dutchman who always calls at about seven o'clock in the morning and clears her out completely of anything horsey every time.

The pattern of trade is changing and in consequence her business has to adapt itself to new conditions. At one time being competitive was all that mattered but now catering for the home furnishing demand is important. Small pieces of furniture are in demand if they are cheaper than those available in shops. Frances has developed a trade for small pieces of stripped pine, like medicine chests, hanging shelves, small chests of drawers, mirrors and kitchen sundries such as egg racks and bread boards. There is also a growing call for trendy clothes of the twenties, thirties and forties and a brisk turnover in table linen. But Frances insists that the backbone of her business is still the antiques trade fairs.

John Hoskins

John Hoskins returned from East Africa in 1963 with his wife and son of secondary school age when he, himself, was forty-seven-years-old. Even in those days he felt that there was little chance of securing suitable employment, although there were jobs available on a somewhat lower level than he had been able to command overseas. He therefore decided to buy a gift shop in a provincial town with his severance pay and savings. It had comfortable accommodation above and he and his wife could run the shop together.

After the initial excitement of the first year getting the business on its feet, he found that time hung on his hands and that his wife could easily run the shop for most of the week on her own; he lending a hand only at weekends and times of greatest pressure like Christmas and Easter. He also did most of the buying, visiting wholesalers and trade fairs.

He started visiting auction sales and poking around junk shops in the immediate area to his home and when away on buying trips, picking up the odd interesting item. Some years before, his brother-in-law had established himself as an art dealer in eighteenth and nineteenth century paintings and he encouraged John to develop his talent for repairing and renovating furniture which could be purchased in poor condition for very cheap prices at that time.

He started off buying pieces of potentially good eighteenth century furniture which were in general demand, like chests of drawers, bureaux and desks, dressing-table mirrors, writing slopes, tea caddies, knife boxes and the like. Most of the items he bought needed no more than superficial repairs and repolishing, but he also saw the potential of other more badly damaged items in need of more comprehensive restoration.

He met, during his travels, a restorer with a large studio who took in occasional pupils on short courses and went to work in his workshop for a month where he picked up the techniques of professional restoration. He also attended, over the years, a series of short seminars in furniture restoration run by CoSIRA, then on Wimbledon Common.

For at least a decade John earned a living by buying from one auction, making the item presentable and then selling it either in another auction or to a dealer. This taught him that you have to be selective over which auction rooms you use for buying and which for selling as values vary widely from one room to the next. Sometimes you can buy in London and sell in the country, sometimes the reverse. During these years he continued to take advantage of the fact that there were always bargains to be picked up in auction rooms that had been overlooked by even the porters and bought for 'investment' and for his own pleasure, whenever the opportunity arose.

Over the years the trade changed and quality furniture, even in a poor state, became so expensive that there was little or no profit in buying and restoring it to put back in auction. He therefore started to do more and more restoration for private collectors and the trade. He also found he could turn over his 'investment' collection at a useful profit by offering it to shops specialising in the things he had collected and studied, mainly eighteenth century English pottery and prints of transport subjects, particularly railways and stagecoaches.

He still spent a considerable part of his time in auction rooms and at country house sales where, John says, there are still plenty of bargains if you keep your eyes and ears open.

At a house sale, just a few weeks before this interview was recorded, he purchased two lots in the 'effects and junk' section of the auction when it had just started and before the big dealers, who anyway were only interested in the important furniture and silver, arrived. One mixed lot he bought for £5.00 because it included a carboy which he knew he could sell immediately at a profit. The lot was coupled with the previous lot, lodged in the cellar, for which the auctioneer had been unable to raise a bid. When, after the sale, he investigated it he found he had bought a large iron-bound oak silver chest which when polished up fetched £40.00 in auction; a Doulton wash hand basin which had been used for mixing cement he cleaned up and sold for £8.50; two large glass vases which auctioned for £9.00; a load of miscellaneous effects which sold as a separate lot for £6.00; and a good little framed watercolour which he kept for himself. A total of £69.50 and a profit of £64.50, less half a day spent on cleaning.

The second lot was a collection of sea shells which he bought on spec, also for a fiver. It included eight drawers from a specimen cabinet — but no cabinet to hold them. The shells he advertised in the Shell Collectors Club Newsletter and sold for £15.00 over the phone. He built a cabinet incorporating the eight mahogany-fronted drawers which sold at auction for £75.00 (less 15 per cent auctioneer's commission ie £63.75), having spent just over a day constructing the cabinet. A gross profit of £78.75 plus £64.50 equals £143.25.

John says that this kind of luck does not come along very often, and when it does you have to be able to recognise the potential quickly as the auctioneer won't wait for you to make up your mind. However, it happens often enough to put some spice into looking for bargains. Inspite of heavy motoring expenses he makes a very comfortable living and leads a life free from frustration as he can please himself when and where he goes to work. He looks on what he does as serious work and still spends time reading and studying the specialities that interest him most, as well as reading generally about antiques. He doubts if he will ever retire completely as he is enjoying himself so much, although these days he takes life fairly easily.

Patricia Ellis

Pat Ellis started buying antiques when she married, back in 1948. Her husband was a farmer and all their capital had been invested in stock and equipment for the farm. She says that they were very hard up and their furniture consisted largely of 'family throwouts' with which she intended to live for as short a time as possible. This was just about the time that they stopped selling utility furniture and, as they could not afford new, Pat started to improve her home by selling off what she did not want and buying good-quality secondhand which, at the time, was literally going for a song. She wistfully remembers that on one occasion she bought six Regency chairs, a dining set in almost perfect condition, for five pounds.

She was very friendly with two old ladies who kept an antique shop in the neighbouring town, neither of whom could drive a car, so she used to take them out on buying expeditions in her husband's car. This experience she feels, on looking back, was invaluable to her as the two ladies were very knowledgeable and they taught her a great deal about recognising good antiques when she saw them. As they grew older and less mobile and Pat became acquainted with what she was doing she started buying on their behalf and later, when one of the ladies fell ill, she helped out in their shop. Eventually one of her friends died and she took over the shop completely for about six months until the nephew who had inherited the estate was able to dispose of it.

By this time she had a family and recalls that she used to take the babies with her in the back of the car when out on buying excursions. Because she was now well-known in the trade and to private buyers and sellers in the district, she had no difficulty in transferring her business to the front room of the farmhouse. She found it was no great problem, under these circumstances, to cope with three small children and dealing at the same time, as she was largely home-based.

One of the most useful lessons she had learned from her old friends was to haggle and never to accept the price at which an article was first offered. She says that you can do this in a polite manner without embarrassment if you think about what you are going to say before you say it and keep your cool. Her experience with them also helped her to develop a good business-sense and an ability to assess values.

Having inherited the old ladies' connections, she sold a lot to the antique trade as well as to locals, but she recalls that while her family were young she did not rely on the trade as a living. It was more of a hobby which kept her alert and gave her an interest outside the home environment. She says that she loved every minute of it and that although money was tight, the profits from her business provided the cost of a good private education for her children and kept them clothed during their schooldays.

As their farm was situated near one of the main horse dealing and training areas of the country, part of her husband's farming activity was dealing in, transporting and stabling horses. This brought her into contact with many of the people who circulated in the horsey world, both those with above-average incomes and the gypsies and travelling people who had big money to spend. The gypsies were particularly good customers, for they are among the keenest connoisseurs of Crown Derby porcelain and Pat developed a fondness for many of them with whom she could trade, both buying and selling the porcelain that they loved and other things like gold jewellery and brass and copper.

Patricia maintains that quality sells every time so she has always dealt only in the best. She has never had to advertise due to the fortunate nature of her husband's business, and she attributes her success to always trying to have what people want and searching for things asked for by her customers. She maintains that, once established, word of mouth and reputation for fairness and honesty is enough to keep a business going. She admits it can be frustrating when, having searched and found something for a customer, the article is refused, but, she says, she never bought anything that would not sell by itself. The gypsies were the best for sticking to their bargains once made and the habit of giving 'luck money', or more often in her case a luck present, provided her with some of the most treasured pieces in her extensive private collection.

Ten years ago she and her husband left the farm and went to live in the nearby town. As a result she did not have so many callers and needed a new outlet. This she has found by having strategically placed displaycases in several hotel foyers and these now provide the bulk of her trade. She says that she is continually amazed at the rate of turnover.

The week before she had sold a £400.00 watch, two antique rings, two porcelain figures and several small boxes.

For this trade you must pick hotels in the three to five-star bracket and concentrate on pretty things which are suitable for gifts, such as good porcelain, quality small silver, jewellery, dressing-table ornaments, candlesticks, powder and trinket bowls and boxes, silver and pewter mugs. You must stock the cabinets with the kind of thing that stimulates impulse buying and pitch the price to suit the pockets of the visitors.

Pat's sources of supply are mainly old friends in the trade who know the kinds of things she likes best. As she has lived in the same area most of her life she is well-known and feels that most of the articles being sold privately are offered to her. She also has the chance of a house clearance two or three times a year; this she can take on with the help of her son and a few local lads anxious to earn some money to see them through college or to buy a motor bike. She says that there are still loads of antiques and 'objets de virtue' around in people's homes, if only you can get the chance to buy them when households are selling up.

Directory of Suppliers

One of the problems encountered when undertaking renovations is finding the correct materials for repairs. The first resort is to the yellow pages of the telephone directory, for in Britain we are fortunate in having a large number of craft suppliers distributed throughout the country. In addition the list given below is a selection of firms who specialise in various commodities that are not likely to be found in the average ironmonger or DIY shop. Where the firm does mail order the letters 'MO' precede the address.

The list is by no means exhaustive; for a more comprehensive directory consult *Studio Vista Guide to Craft Suppliers*.

Barometers
Garner & Marney Ltd
41 Southgate Road
London N1

Bookbinding supplies
MO Russell Bookcrafts
Bancroft
Hitchin, Herts

J. Hewitt & Sons
97 St John Street
London EC1

Brass castings
MO Escare Metal Co Ltd
195 Bexhill Road
St Leonards on Sea

Brass handles and fittings
J.D. Beardmore Ltd
1-3 Percy Street
London W1

MO John Lawrence & Co Ltd
Granville Street
Dover

MO Messrs H. E. Saville
Sunwood
Weaponness Park
Scarborough

Brass inlay, strip and sheet
Smith & Son Ltd
42-52 St John Square
London EC1

Cane and rush for seating
MO Dryad
   Northgates
   Leicester

MO Crafts Unlimited
   178 Kensington High Street
   London W8

Carving tools and chisels
MO Ashley Iles (Edge Tools) Ltd
   East Kirkby
   Spilsbury, Leics

MO Henry Taylor
   Rutland Road
   Sheffield S3 9NP

MO Alec Tiranti Ltd
   70 High Street
   Theale, Berks

Chain burnishers
   T. Marten & Sons Ltd
   Bridgeman Street
   Walsall, Staffs

French polish
   Furniglas Ltd
   136 Great North Road
   Hatfield, Herts

French polishing sundries
MO Gedge & Co Ltd
   88 St John Street
   London EC1

MO Henry Flack Ltd
   Croydon Road
   Beckenham, Kent

MO Fiddes & Son
   Trade Street
   Cardiff

Gilding supplies and leaf
MO E. Ploton (Sundries) Ltd
   273 Archway Road
   London N6

MO Geo. Whiley Ltd
   Victoria Road
   South Ruislip
   Middlesex

Horsehair fabrics
MO Messrs John Boyd
   Castle Cary
   Somerset

Leather
MO Grainwave Enterprises
   15 Clifton Gardens
   London N15

Leather tools
MO Taylor & Co Ltd
   54 Old Street
   London EC1

Metal polishing materials
MO T.A. Hutchinson Ltd
   16 St Johns Lane
   London EC1

Mirrors (antiqued)
    Semnat Glass Ltd
    73 Hackney Road
    London E7

Music box repairs and parts
MO Keith Harding Ltd
    93 Hornsey Road
    London N7

Picture framing materials
MO Handicrafts (Peter-
    borough) Ltd
    New Road
    Peterborough

Stringing (wood)
MO Crispin & Son Ltd
    92 Curtain Road
    London EC2

Table leathers
MO Antique Leathers Ltd
    4 Park End
    South Hill Park
    Pont Street
    London NW3

MO Beal & Partners
    2 Whites Grounds
    Bermondsey Street
    London SE1

MO R. Clements Upholstery
    50 Fullers Road
    London E15

Tapestry
MO Arthur Lee & Son
    Stanley Road
    Birkenhead, Cheshire

Upholstery supplies
MO Mobilia
    44 Henniker Road
    Stratford
    London E15

Veneers, inlays
MO Crispin & Son Ltd
    92 Curtain Road
    London E2

Wood and woodworking requisite
MO World of Wood
    Industrial Estate
    Mildenhall
    Suffolk

Bibliography

Price Guides

Millers Antiques Price Guide (published by MJM Publications, Pugins Hall, Finchden Manor, Tenterden, Kent. Tel 058 062234

The Lyle Antiques Review (Glenmayne, Galashields, Selkirkshire, Scotland)

Price Guide to Antique Furniture (published by The Antique Collectors Club, 5 Church St, Woodbridge, Suffolk. Tel. 039 43 5501) This publisher also has a large range of specialised guides including:
Eighteenth Century English Pottery
Eighteenth and Nineteenth Century British Porcelain
Old Sheffield Plate
Goss Miniatures
Victorian Furniture
Collectable Antiques

There are at any one time many hundreds of books in print on various aspects of antique collecting. For comprehensive lists apply to:

The Antiques Book Centre
93 Bradmore Green
Brookmans Park
Hatfield
Herts AL9 7QT
Tel. 0707 44426

Stobart & Son Ltd
67-73 Worship St
London EC2A 2EL
Tel. 01-247 8671

Glossary

AF Meaning 'As Found'. Usually seen in auction catalogues denoting that the article is so badly damaged that it was not worthwhile trying to conceal the fact.

Bent Usually this means stolen, or at any rate that there is something not quite 'straight' or honest about it.

Brassed Up When a piece of furniture has had wooden handles removed and brass ones substituted, brass embellishments and even stringing added to make it appear more appealing to the buyer. This practice was very common when the Italians could afford to come to Britain to buy.

Callout When a dealer is invited to go to someone's house with a view to purchasing the entire contents or even just an item or two, this is known as a callout and is greeted with jubilation as there is not likely to be any competition.

Clean Without any visible flaw. It is as well to look carefully for the invisible ones.

Crud The dregs of a clearance or any other collection of junk that may come your way.

Cut This may have several meanings, but in particular you may hear someone say that a chest of drawers or some other item has been cut. They mean that it has been cut down, perhaps that the bottom drawer has been removed and the legs stuck back on to make a lower and more acceptable piece of furniture.

Dateline In the better antiques fairs a dateline is set for each class of article and nothing manufactured more recently than the date set is allowed in the show.

Drink A sum of money given to somebody for rendering assistance. A polite way of asking for a tip, eg 'All I want is a drink out of it'.

EPBM Electroplated Brittania Metal.

EPNS Electroplated Nickel Silver.

Gear This means stock or articles to sell. *Bent gear* is stolen property.

Jappo-di-Monte The name given to Japanese copies of Capo-di-Monte figures and groups.

Jockey A courier engaged by a foreign buyer to guide him round the best antique shops, often supplied by export packers and shippers. They usually require a percentage so offer one if you want to see them a second time.

Kitsch Outre, vulgar or over-decorated. Pandering to popular bad taste. Goods only disposable in a limited field.

Knocker An itinerant dealer who knocks on doors to try and talk the unsuspecting into selling their treasures.

Knockout The illegal auction held after an auction sale by members of the 'Ring'. After refraining from bidding against each other in a legitimate auction sale, dealers meet together to sell articles bought cheaply among themselves at somewhere near the true value. The proceeds are divided between the members of the ring.

Lump A very large piece of furniture that is difficult to move is often referred to as a lump.

Marriage When two pieces of furniture are put together to make a more valuable single item this is known as a marriage, eg putting a bookcase on top of a bureau to make a bureau-bookcase.

No trade left in it   When an article has changed hands among dealers so many times that the only way to dispose of it is to find a retail customer.

Punter A customer.

Petrol money   Another word for a tip or for payment for the provision of some service.

Runner   An itinerant dealer who trades from a van by buying from one dealer and selling to another. You can use runners to advantage to find new sources of the kind of article that you particularly want.

Ring   An illegal association of dealers who refrain from bidding against each other at auction sales.

Repro   A reproduction of an antique.

Running up   At auction sales another dealer will sometimes run up the price of an article to discourage competition, discourage a new dealer from coming to subsequent auctions or similar reasons. Auctioneers also like to speed up the pace of bidding when there is keen rivalry for an article as it encourages the unsuspecting to pay more than they intended.

Shipper   A dealer who stuffs containers with antiques and ships them overseas.

Smalls   Any small article other than furniture, carpets and pictures.

Tarted up   This refers to anything, but especially furniture, that has had the minimum of renovation and polishing done to make it saleable.

Turn it up   When a dealer asks if he can turn it up, he wants to look at the underside and back of a piece of furniture.

Index

Health and Fitness for the Over Forties

Health and Fitness for the Over Forties

Bill Watson

STANLEY PAUL, LONDON

Stanley Paul & Co Ltd
3 Fitzroy Square, London W1

An imprint of the Hutchinson Publishing Group

London Melbourne Sydney Auckland
Wellington Johannesburg Cape Town
and agencies throughout the world

First published 1975
© Bill Watson 1975
Drawings © Stanley Paul & Co Ltd 1975

Set in Monotype Baskerville
Printed in Great Britain by The Anchor Press Ltd
and bound by Wm Brendon & Son Ltd
both of Tiptree, Essex

ISBN 0 09 121240 5 (cased)
       0 09 121241 3 (paper)

Contents

Foreword

This book is about fitness – not the super-fitness of athletes and superstars – but the everyday and essential fitness that each individual needs for his own well-being. And let me stress right away that no matter how hopeless you may feel, whatever physical shape you may be in, or whatever your age, you can always improve your health, strength and your figure. The guidance you need is in this book.

I am sure you will be able to follow my simple but effective systems and, by way of encouragement, let me recommend my own example.

In 1941, when hundreds of thousands of incendiary bombs were raining down and London seemed to be ablaze, I happened to be home on leave. An incendiary fell in my back garden, setting fire to the fence. I threw sandbags on the bomb but it suddenly exploded, throwing me against a wall ten feet away. My uniform was partly blown off, my body and hair badly burned, and my eyes damaged. Later, in 1942, when I was still in the Services, I was crushed between an army truck and a wall and my feet were badly maimed. This time I was discharged as medically unfit for any sort of duty!

In both these cases I recovered and trained myself

back to health, becoming in the process a keen devotee of fitness, largely through weight-lifting. In fact I even succeeded in becoming the British middleweight champion in this sport, and achieved the distinction of competing in the 1948 Olympic Games. In recent years I have become better known in sporting circles for my training methods, and as trainer at three of the country's top First Division soccer clubs.

It is important to remember that the body is the most valuable possession we have, and should be treasured as such. Age alone need not affect your general standard of fitness. Mae West, who is eighty-one, still uses 15-lb dumb-bells, bicycle exercises and walking machines to keep in shape. Victor Silvester, at an age when most people have retired, can be seen at a London gymnasium keeping himself in condition with fairly heavy weights. These are two people whose vitality and zest for life is attributable in no small way to their fitness, and I am sure that with determination you will find my analysis and methods both beneficial and rewarding.

It never ceases to amaze me that so many simple and fundamental elements of fitness are constantly overlooked. One of the first exercises deals with breathing, and I think you will see that, on the whole, we do not breathe at all correctly. Indeed, we are a nation of shallow breathers, and you will understand why as you read on. Another vital issue that tends to be treated casually is the need for a balanced diet. In today's fast-moving world, I am convinced that much of the ill-health that is so prevalent is due to the little awareness we have of such factors – we simply do not consistently eat wholesome food, and neither do we use our lungs as we should.

Sickness comes as a surprise to many people, and they are probably the very ones who underestimate the tremendous significance of fitness in their lives. For instance, a common ailment which keeps about 50 000 people off work every day is backache. This alone costs industry something like £100 million per year in lost production – about £7 a year for the average worker. The problem is so serious that the Arthritis and Rheumatism Council last year allocated £57 000 to backache research. . . . Little wonder that the old 'grandmother's funeral' excuse for absenteeism has been replaced with the backache excuse!

Backache will be fully discussed in later chapters, but the softness of our lives in the modern, push-button era is almost certainly one of the chief causes of this painful and niggling complaint, which in its extreme form has become an osteopath's nightmare. Of course, one should always take great care when lifting any object, and physical work should be taken in easy stages. It is most important to pace oneself, and guard against the over-enthusiasm which can send you blindly into the first gardening chores of the year. But the simplest and most effective way to prevent back trouble is just to keep fit. And if you rely wholly on planes, cars, escalators and lifts then you will miss out on one of the most effective of all forms of exercise – walking.

What I propose to do in this book is to show you how to recognize and combat the various health hazards which exist today, and in so doing I hope that *Health and Fitness for the Over Forties* will play a part in saving this country a great deal of wasted time and money.

PART I

Introduction

Does Life Begin at Forty?

The answer to the question 'Does life begin at forty?' is that it most certainly can if you, the middle-aged reader at whom this book is aimed, tackle things the correct and simple way. At the age of forty one tends to take stock of oneself. Young people are inclined to abuse themselves to some extent. After all, they are virile, active and young. Life doesn't carry the same tensions, strains and stresses.

Maybe the average forty-year-old is too much of a worrier. Perhaps he worries over his increasing waistline (and she does the same, not to mention the wrinkles too). Mr Forty may also be worried over the increase in heart diseases and his own lessening of sporting activity.

Concern, not worry, over these factors is a better attitude. And moderation should be your watchword when it comes to activity.

The main purpose of my book is to persuade you to build up a home exercise programme that will, if properly applied, keep you fit, healthy and in good shape. When it comes to other activity it is important to remember not to over-exercise and otherwise overdo things. Think of the man who rushes out to tackle his large garden. He goes to work as though he hasn't a minute to live – and so often ends in trouble.

Then there is the belief, in my opinion greatly mistaken, that golf and squash keep you fit. From America come more and more reports of middle-aged and elderly men falling fatally ill through over-indulgence in such strenuous activities as squash. This ill-planned exuberance in tackling such exhausting sports as squash, cycling, running, swimming or tennis, causes far more trouble than it should. Far better, in my view, as a beneficial activity is walking, as I have prescribed in another chapter.

If you must tackle other more strenuous activities please remember to use moderation and, if you are, for example, working in the garden, just do a little at a time.

You might also remember the words of the American movie star James Cagney, who for his age is a model of health and well-being. He once said: 'The secret of my success in keeping fit is never to take my heart by surprise.' He was, of course, a dancer all his life and was keeping in trim even in his seventies by a little dancing each day, taking a few steps to limber up.

Do not take your heart by surprise: a worthwhile motto that must be stressed, when you begin your life at forty.

The Question of Longevity

Longevity is much talked about in these enlightened days. But it has been said with a degree of wisdom that the real problem of longevity is not so much how long man can live but whether he is willing to make the effort – or whether society will permit him. My firm belief is that exercise and the right kind of diet are the paramount factors. This indeed, basically, is what my book is all about.

Numerous studies with animals have revealed interesting facts. The results show that eating less and sleeping more favour longevity. Evidence suggests that this basic law also applies to humans.

The over-eaters are unquestionably more prone to organic malfunctioning and breakdown – heart and coronary disease and digestive disorders especially. In a nut shell, Western man has succeeded in increasing his potential life-span by removing severe environmental hazards and improving hygiene and general living standards, but, at the same time, ever-increasing mechanization is causing him to use his body less and less. In view of this drop in physical activity, and the increased food consumption, with people eating solely for pleasure, the overall picture is less encouraging.

'Trendy' foods often cause deterioration and reduced efficiency in the body-structure and internal organs.

Sedentary man has become physically softer, and probably has fewer resources to cope with the continual invasion of bacteria, viruses and toxins. Hence his growing reliance on artificially-produced chemicals and drugs. Manual workers, on the other hand, may use their exterior motor muscles, but often overload their digestive and excretory systems. So the average labouring manual worker, instead of being naturally lean and athletic, is more often than not overburdened with excess fat and toxic deposits. In brief, his intake exceeds his output.

The real answer lies in self-discipline in reducing the amount we eat. Also, more sleep is needed to reduce the stress of our competitive existence. Eat less, exercise and relax more...that is good, sound common sense!

Statistics invariably show that men's life-spans tend to be shorter than women's. A number of reasons can be put forward for this fact. For example, there are thousands of men who try to prove their manhood by over-exerting themselves, even when they don't feel well. Considered, as they are, to be the stronger sex, they have always been expected to do the hard work, to fight, to hunt. This might have been in order generations ago, but frankly too many men are not fit enough today to tackle certain things.

Take a simple job like shovelling snow or digging the garden. More often than not the unfit man will do such work after eating a big meal. Is it any wonder that his heart will be hard-pressed to keep the blood circulating to digest the food, as well as to maintain the body-temperature needed to carry out a heavy and often unaccustomed job? Then there is the man who races through breakfast (often eating food of little nourishment) and then, discovering he is late for work, frequently has to run to catch a bus or train. Again is it any wonder that damage to the heart is likely, eventually shortening his life-span?

The argument about whether men or women are the stronger is never-ending. Quite honestly, there should be no real difference, although, medically speaking, it seems that women live on average eight years longer. It is a widespread view that men will carry on working until they fall ill, in order not to show weakness, while women more sensibly take a break if they feel tired, or get help if they face a job they cannot do. Women are also said to have greater endurance.

It is a fact that, inevitably, the years will pass, and no one can prevent the process of growing old. But what we can all do is to try to remain young in mind and in behaviour.

For a man who insists on proving that he has not lost his masculine toughness, the answer is simply to learn how to strengthen himself and keep in shape. Otherwise the chores he tackles can be extremely harmful. So be prepared, watch your diet, and exercise the muscles properly. Always remember, too, that the natural foods are best. In our quest for a long life-span these must be the overriding factors.

B

Developing a Tranquil Mind

One of the four essentials of good health is a tranquil mind. Never has this been more vital than today when, despite the tremendous progress of medicine, mental pressures seem to grow all the time. That is why developing a tranquil mind is so necessary. This simply means the ability to keep calm, to keep cool, and not allow things to bother or worry you. It is not easy, I admit. For thousands of car-commuters in a niggling traffic-jam in the rush-hour keeping cool is very hard. But it can be done.

There is no doubt at all that worry, anger, hatred and jealousy can injure one's health. It is common emotions like these that produce nervous indigestion, nervous exhaustion and headaches. Indigestion is high on my list of health hazards. Elsewhere I have explained the enormous benefits of eating a good wholesome meal in pleasant surroundings or in convivial company. In such circumstances, the process of digestion will proceed rapidly and smoothly.

But consider a situation where, for example, the meal is badly cooked and badly balanced; where nagging goes on at the family table; or when one is obsessed and on edge about things going badly in business or at home. In a situation like this you are, frankly, better off not to eat at all, for your digestion is bound to be greatly affected.

A conclusive weight of opinion suggests that much of today's sickness results, one way or another, from indigestion and constipation. So, calmness and tranquillity when eating are essential in the quest for health and fitness.

The connection between mental and physical well-being has never been more marked than today. This connection is seen in the fact that many nervous, edgy people are thin and under-nourished, while, in contrast, the happy, good-natured individual is frequently plump. Of course, as I shall stress in another chapter, being fat is no state to strive for. In some cases, this may be due to good digestion and assimilation, but in many others, it is frankly the result of laziness. The simple answer is to avoid fat-forming foods and cultivate exercise and activity.

Really healthy people tend to be easy-going. Do they become healthy because of that happy mental state, or do they become easy-going as a result of their invigorating health! The two factors are of course complementary to each other.

Another equally serious health barrier is nervous exhaustion. Normal fatigue brought about by normal exertion, whether through work or exercise, usually disappears after a good night's sleep. But, if an individual habitually does not get enough rest, nervous exhaustion will result – a state in which you feel completely lethargic; it is indeed a sorry business. One of the worst things you can do is to keep going when you feel tired or off-colour. This imposes a great nervous strain and upsets the body-process. In fact it is a vicious circle. When you are tired it takes more nerve-power to keep going, and this results in more tiredness, aches and pains – and more exhaustion.

The remedies lie mainly in sufficient sound sleep and a regulation of your life. Organize your work so that you never become overtired and utterly exhausted. If your work seems too hard for you there are two alternatives: give it up or regulate your life accordingly. Nor will temporary lifts from stimulants provide the answer. Habit-forming stimulants such as drugs, alcohol and tobacco will simply rob the body's store-houses of their supply of glycogen or muscle-fuel. It is like the chap who gets drunk at a party. At the time he feels great – but that awful hangover the next morning is the penalty.

Finally, we come to nervous prostration – the serious condition which results from unusual worry and overall fatigue. I don't need to remind you of the number of people who suffer these tragic nervous breakdowns. My advice can only be to develop that calmness, however difficult you might believe this is. Think! How many times has a problem which seemed to loom so darkly one day been forgotten in a week?

Tranquillity of mind comes partially from environment but mainly from practice. Determination and self-denial should be cultivated. Aim to be positive and promise yourself not to let worry, anger, envy and hate invade your being. At the same time look for real interests, work and hobbies, one of the very best hobbies being exercise and physical training.

Finally always remember – keep your cool!

Fresh Air and Sunlight

Fresh air and sunlight are synonymous with health and well-being. One hears a lot today about air-pollution, and I agree with reformists when it comes to this vexed question. The smoke and smog that impair our big towns and cities are a shocking problem. Something really will have to be done to cleanse the air and atmosphere. Nor do car fumes do anything to help. Lucky are those in this modern age who live in what is left of the unspoiled countryside. It is not that I am against progess. But I cannot over-emphasize the importance of getting as much fresh air and sunlight as we possibly can.

There is absolutely no question that it is ultra-violet rays which provide the greatest benefit to health, principally because of their influence on the utilization of phosphorus and calcium. This is the way vitamin D is primarily formed, produced by the action of the rays upon certain oils in the skin. Other effects are an increase in the white corpuscles of the blood which overcome disease germs. The stimulating effects of these sun-rays have many times been proved and tested on plants and animals. You can see for yourself the superior growth of plants on the sunny side of a house as compared with the shady side.

Briefly, sunlight improves the function of the skin, stimulating the sweat glands and evaporating water from the surface of the body. With its absorption, the body can better resist disease and infection, and un-developed muscle tissue is also repaired. It is a big help towards maintaining condition and keeping physically fit, and obviously out-of-doors – in the country, in the mountains or by the sea – is the best place to reap maxi-mum benefit, because in many of our big cities and towns ultra-violet rays are filtered out by smoke and moisture in the air.

A word of warning, however, about the hazards of too much sunshine. If the body is exposed for too long there is danger of blistering and the destruction of tissue. Moderate exposure, on the other hand, produces a feeling of comfort, warmth and relaxation. For those who wish to sunbathe and tan, the main thing to remember is to proceed gradually. Start with five minutes only and slowly increase by five minutes each day. A good suntan lotion and dark glasses are ad-visable, and remember to cover the head from time to time, and also to cool off occasionally in the shade.

Walking for Health

Walking is an activity which has been with us since man took his first step. And it will probably be with us until man takes his final step. Its importance for our health is absolutely vital. Many great men, including statesmen and world leaders, have been devoted walkers. And it is certainly true that many people have solved their problems or developed their ideas and plans while walking.

From the health and fitness angle, which is our concern here, it is of paramount importance. In these days of swift, easy and readily available transport we are, alas, unhappily becoming a nation of armchair travellers. But, walking is clearly our most simple and natural attribute. We are all walkers, although the vast majority of us are what I call 'short walkers'.

We walk, perhaps, ten feet across the kitchen or the office and ten feet back. Probably most of us clock up two or three miles a day in such a manner, depending on our employment. You may ask: 'Why shouldn't this provide enough exercise in itself?' The answer lies in inertia. To put it simply, before we can take a step the inertia of gravity must be overcome. Many stops and starts mean therefore that one must battle with this inertia. That is why at the end of a day so many people have aching legs and feet.

The real value of walking to our health is in the flow of motion and movement and correct breathing. The body should stretch out and stride along with a smooth rhythm. After a while a regular rhythm is set up, and the muscles feel relaxed instead of being tensed and bunched. A good example of inertia is when you walk with a small child or a dog at your side. Having to move at a slow dawdling pace can be much more tiring than walking briskly.

The breathing and posture side of walking needs to be stressed. I suggest five steps to one slow inhale and exhale. Then build up to ten steps. Keep the chest up and the head back and do not stoop. This brings the arms and shoulders into action and increases chest-mobility. One of the great advantages of walking is that the body observes its own posture fairly well. If you keep the head erect and bend the knees slightly instead of walking straight-legged, the feet will take the weight of the body evenly. The best policy is just to relax. After trying the walking exercise I have outlined, for a short while, you will definitely find your stamina and your lung capacity improved.

Walking should be a vital part of your overall fitness programme. Nature gave us this natural process, but early man needed to run when he chased or was being chased by some adversary or foe. Perhaps the truth is that since then we have always been running rather than walking – both with our minds and on wheels – we tend to forget that our natural wheels are our legs.

A word or two on footwear and the best places to walk. A firm comfortable pair of shoes, flat or low-heeled are best. Do not walk in slippers which spread the feet. The shoes should be flexible and wide enough not to cramp the toes together. Cotton socks are good to wear for they absorb moisture. If you can, avoid walking on the pavement, because a hard surface jars the feet. Uneven ground is good for ankles and feet and should be sought, and, naturally, parks or country fields are ideal.

Depending on your job and circumstances you will obviously exercise-walk when you can, but early morning and late in the evening are particularly good times. The air then is fresh and pure and free from car fumes, and those of you who are retired will have little difficulty in making use of this period of the day or night. Incidentally, many retired people are among the best walkers I know. They set an example to younger people; and so can you.

Walking helps to remove nervous tension. Once you have left the busy city streets, and got away from all forms of traffic, your nervous system can begin to relax, and that alone makes walking a healthy tonic. Walking also promotes the circulation, ridding the body of toxic elements, and the abdominal muscles are affected by the action of the legs.

Headaches are sometimes due to weak feet, which distort the natural position of the spine and cause nerve-pressure. The more you walk the sooner you will discover that strong feet can do more to relieve your headaches than any chemist's pill.

How to Sleep Soundly and Well

We spend a third of our lives sleeping. Now there is a sobering thought! But although considerable studies have been made into the magic of sleep, it remains one of the biggest mysteries of all time. However, it is a known fact that it is a great healer of disease. Tissues of the body recuperate during sleep from the chemical changes that have been going on during the hours of activity. It is then that broken-down tissue is replaced.

Exactly how much sleep is required by the average person varies according to age, vocation and mode of living. Some people sleep less than others, awaking utterly refreshed after a period which would leave others still tired. Generally speaking, for middle-aged people the hours of midnight to 7.00 a.m. are sufficient for most needs. Older people require more.

Let's take a look at the sleeping habits of some of the great men of history and of some famous sportsmen.

Napoleon is said to have possessed the ability to sleep at any time, closing his mind to what was going on around him. A sportsman with the same aptitude was the well-known heavyweight boxer of yesteryear, Gene Tunney. The story goes that, before his memorable world-title fight with Jack Dempsey (which he won),

Tunney slept in his dressing-room until called. By contrast Dempsey was in a constant state of nerves and using up nervous energy. So it wasn't surprising that he lost when fight-time came round.

There is little doubt that sleep is best induced through physical effort. During sleep the lost energy and worn tissue are not only replaced but also a greater supply, capable of still more power, is built up. On the other hand, there is no doubt that too much sleep provides no benefits. On the contrary, it causes sluggishness. What we need is plenty of deep sleep, and the brain needs it even more than the body.

There are thousands of people in the country who spend millions of pounds each year on sleeping-pills and powders. It goes without saying that such things should, if possible, be completely avoided. It is far better to let work and exercise induce normal fatigue.

My health programme for sleep follows a series of elementary rules. First and foremost there is the often discussed question of whether to eat before retiring.

A warm drink of, say, malted milk, or some light food will generally stimulate sleep. But a heavy meal will, to a greater or lesser extent, disturb the slumber. For, obviously, no one can sleep with severe indigestion and this is something that can so easily result from the so-called 'bedtime snack'. Also to be avoided are coffee (caffeine is a drug that keeps one awake), alcohol or tobacco.

The time when most people go to sleep varies according to circumstances and temperament. The old saying that two hours' sleep before midnight is of greater value than four afterwards really cannot be accepted. For some people are at their best late at night, while others function better in the morning.

It is a sad thought that today there are more insomnia sufferers than ever. To some extent this is a result of the high-pressure, tension-ridden world we have to live in, for an enormous part of the inability to sleep lies in the mind. And the biggest enemies are mental unrest, worry, fear and anger. If someone has a problem on his mind, a financial worry, perhaps, or an argument, then it is only too likely that sleep will not come as the events of the day are turned over and over in the mind.

What is the answer? Well, there are ways which can help you gain that precious sleep. Try reading yourself to sleep, for example. Keep stray thoughts out of your mind, slowly close your eyes as you read, and soon you should be able to sleep.

Then there is the use of sound. The lullaby of a mother rocking her baby to a nursery theme is the oldest example of this. But for an adult the sound of a radio turned down low could be sufficient. Other essential factors are a comfortable bed and a well-ventilated bedroom – a room with space for cool, fresh air to circulate is a big advantage. And many people cover themselves with too much bedclothing.

Perfect relaxation is the real secret – and keeping to a happy medium. Remember, moderation in all things. Just as too much work, or too much play, is not good for you, neither is too much sleep. My main rules are: exercise in the early evening, a warm bath, a warm drink, and the dropping of all cares and worries. Not wasting too much of your time in bed allows you to live longer. That is a known fact.

So, happy dreams.

The Question of Virility

When you read the chapter entitled 'Does Life Begin at Forty', you may have wondered why I never discussed the vital question of sexual virility. The reason is simple – it is such an important subject that it needs a separate chapter to itself. There has long been an outdated myth that sex belongs exclusively to the younger generation, and that when a man or woman reaches the age of forty this integral part of one's life just wanes away or disappears. Nothing is further from the truth.

A happy, well-balanced relationship is a very significant factor in a couple's general health and fitness. This connects with the chapter in which I stressed the need for a tranquil mind and the removal of worry, stress and strain. When you are burdened by anxiety and fear your physical being is affected.

There are regrettably hundreds of men (some not even forty yet) who have damaging fears that they either have already lost, or will lose, their sexual potency. Likewise, women, especially when they reach the age when the care of their figures becomes an important factor, suffer mental strain, and are often unhappy and miserable over the physical side of their marriage.

The problems connected with such a complex subject are varied, but in this book I am only dealing with one aspect – the need to keep in good physical and mental shape, and the right diet. From this angle sex can be happily enjoyed long after that forty mark, the crucial age that seems to lurk like some secret curse at the back of so many people's minds. There are many doctors who stress that a happy married sex life is synonymous with good health and fitness. Life is physical, and it naturally follows that in most cases the stronger you are physically the greater your sex urge and capacity. But it goes without saying that there must be some exceptions.

Generally speaking, the golden rule is to maintain the right sort of exercise and keep-fit programme in an age when everyday life for many has tended to become unathletic or soft.

There are some American scientists who predict that with the number of labour-saving devices growing yearly, impotency will become an increasingly serious problem over the next decade or two. They may well be right. Certainly I feel that every individual should recognize the importance of the matter and arm himself with a certain amount of health and fitness knowledge.

There can, of course, be no magical tricks bestowing superhuman ability. A tremendous amount of nonsense, too, is written about certain foods as sex-stimulants. The truth is, there has never been proof of a single known food acting as an aphrodisiac. Many of the superstitions may have some factual support, but only because certain foods have the correct basis of nutritional vitamins. You probably know of the superstitious belief that eggs, oysters, clams, red peppers and chilli powder – to name only a few – will instantly act as sexual stimulants. It is said that Casanova was very fond of a salad of egg-whites. These foods may bring about greater vigour if there is a vitamin lack, but the real answer lies in the importance of vitamins B and E, and a well-rounded diet. In this respect eggs (protein) and seafood (iodine) are most beneficial. A good diet for sound physical sexual power would principally consist of various proteins – eggs, fish, beans, milk and liver, for example. This does not mean a constant menu of thick steaks, but a well-varied, moderate diet.

Diet apart, the main factor in the sphere of physical sexual well-being is exercise. My special exercises in this book will be of enormous assistance to you in this respect, and those designed for the ladies with a good figure in mind are no less beneficial. And as regards the right mental approach, you must never, never believe the fallacy that a happy sex-life has to end in middle-age. Often that's when it really begins.

Why Smoke?

One of the biggest killers, it is strongly claimed today, is cigarette smoking. Hence the Government anti-smoking campaigns and, most recently, the warning notices on every packet of cigarettes. In your quest to reach peak fitness you simply cannot afford to ignore this.

The spate of evidence that cigarette smoking can cause lung cancer and lead to heart troubles and bronchitis has been constantly growing. And today it is becoming overwhelming. But long before this evidence was produced I had always been opposed to smoking. Ask yourself honestly, 'How can breathing smoke from a burning weed full of toxics be considered clean, fresh and healthy?' Even if a heavy smoker does not contract lung cancer, he is more prone to coughs and respiratory difficulties. Certainly he is always short of wind.

A lot of the trouble, I personally feel, is that cigarette smoking has become a sort of status symbol. I find it distressing and disturbing to see so many of our youngsters smoking cigarettes as they make their way home from school; I suppose it is considered manly. But parents of course can hardly expect their children to refrain from smoking if they cannot themselves give up the habit.

Let me give you a few facts. There is enough nicotine in a cigar to kill a man. All this nicotine does not get into the body, but obviously a person who inhales smoke absorbs much more of the toxins than does the person who merely puffs. The effects of nicotine on the body are varied. Small amounts will produce a transient stimulation, and increase respiration, blood pressure and muscular sensitivity. The larger amounts which a chain-smoker absorbs will tend to block nervous impulses. It is known to cause constriction of some of the blood-vessels, especially those in the skin – and this may bring on or aggravate many different diseases.

You will have read how, increasingly often, lung cancer is being attributed to heavy smoking, and to the tar content in cigarettes. That the Government is taking the whole business seriously, and that you should too, is shown by their tables of cigarette brands, some containing tar and nicotine in higher quantities than others. My firm advice is to give it up.

The common complaint associated with smoking – shortage of wind – is probably due to an impaired gas-exchange efficiency of the lungs. Simply, this means that the oxygen has a harder time getting in and the carbon-dioxide a more difficult time getting out. This lack of wind may also be the result of a decrease in the oxygen-carrying capacity of the blood. It has been shown that in heavy smokers up to ten per cent of the oxygen-carrying capacity of haemoglobin is tied up by carbon-monoxide from the tobacco smoke. Thus the muscles are deprived of the oxygen fuel that they need.

The first evidence of the effects of heavy smoking came from America, and, ever since, the statistics have pointed more and more to an increase in deaths due to lung cancer. Further, the coronary death-rate is two

C

and a half times higher for smokers than non-smokers.

One well-known American professor of surgery has said, 'It frightens me to think of what is going to happen in another decade when our present smoking habits catch up with us.' He has predicted that by 1977, unless something is done, lung cancer will represent thirty per cent or more of all cancers.

The effects of tar in cigarettes have been measured in America countless times. The tar residue collected from a robot smoking machine was added to a solvent and applied to the skin of animals regularly over a period of time. The solvent alone was applied to the skin of another group of control animals. After two years in the first group forty-four per cent of the animals had died from a metastatic true cancer which had developed at the site of the tar application. But with the other control group there was not one benign or malignant tumour at the end of the same period.

The research results go on, and it is interesting to note that tests show there are virtually no cancer-causing substances in the tar of the smoke when tobacco is burned at 62 °C. This suggests that the way to make cigarettes 'safer', which is a constant topic these days, might be by adding chemicals or by changing the tobacco so that it burns at a lower temperature. Whether or not a so-called 'safe' cigarette is produced remains to be seen. But the truth is that while such a mammoth amount of evidence has been accumulated as to its hazards, it is far better to give up the habit. There are a number of so-called cures on the market, and anti-smoking clinics have been set up to assist the heavy smoker who wants to give it up.

I suppose many people smoke because they do not have the strength and the will-power to follow through with their decision to stop. The habit is enjoyable of course, for a variety of reasons, but can any smoker really say that, in spite of the risk of a shorter life-span, they would rather live a shorter (if more enjoyable) life smoking than a longer life non-smoking?

Other people argue that smoking acts as a lift, like a pep pill, or calms the nerves, or helps to keep down weight. But when it comes to a life of nerves, all drugs in the long run have no lasting benefit. As for loss of weight, smoking does work to some extent as tobacco-smoke depresses the appetite. But my exercises are far more practical, logical, and a sounder basis for reducing weight.

However you look at it, smoking has no part whatsoever in keeping fit and healthy, or leading an active, energetic and lively existence.

The Heart – The Strongest Muscle in the Body

The aim of this book is to make you fit and to keep you fit, and I hope it has an optimistic, happy outlook. I don't like referring to gloomy statistics but from time to time it is necessary. For instance, the biggest killer today is, without a doubt, coronary heart disease. That is why I have devoted a special chapter to the heart – the strongest muscle in the body. It has been estimated that around forty per cent of over-forty men and women have a definite degree of obstruction due to the hardening of the arteries and veins – and this puts them at risk as possible sufferers of some kind of heart problem.

So, a few words about the heart and its vital functions. Have you ever stopped to consider the incredible task the heart has to do to keep you alive and well? This organ is a wonderfully-designed pump whose chief function is to circulate blood to all parts of the body. It pumps about 2,000 gallons of blood every 24 hours, pumping on average 70 times to the minute, and with extra strenuous activity this may increase to 120 times a minute. It is incredible to think that our most powerful and influential organ is about the size of a fist.

To function effectively the heart muscles need a constant supply of energy and nourishment. This comes from oxygen and certain nutrients carried in the blood, which reaches the heart from its own network of arteries, called the coronary arteries. If the supply is restricted we can expect trouble. It may be restricted by, perhaps, a hardening of the arteries, owing to deposits of fat and other material on the inside lining. It is a little like the pipes from a sink becoming rusty through a constant depositing of material.

Simply, the answer is that you must aim to become more active. The more exercise and the more activity, then the more blood pumped through the arteries, making them flexible with the passages open. So my message is: be an active person, not a sitter. Walk, climb, swim, run, skip and dance – do anything in fact to stimulate the blood flow through the circulatory system. As a result your pulse-rate will remain slow, with the stroke volume of the heart sharp and strong.

Building a strong heart can be a vital and rewarding business. The creature comforts of today tend to make people under-exercise and become slaves to television and the car. In fact we are fast becoming a nation of hot-house plants, and this is something we have all got to combat.

I am not suggesting that we all take a cold winter's morning dip in the Serpentine, or dash into the icy waters of Brighton beach on Christmas morning! But I do advocate the cold bath. It is not a shock to the heart and the nervous system (provided that your heart is reasonably strong). On the contrary, it can be a fine aid in maintaining good muscular tone, and improving the circulation and respiration. People who take cold-water baths are not a load of cranks. They know that the stimulation of cool water on the skin produces a condition that forces the blood inward, increasing its supply to the heart and other important parts of the body. Take it in easy stages, and once the initial, mild shock of cold water is over, it is a refreshing experience.

But, whether or not you take cold baths, remember to avoid becoming the typical twentieth-century hot-house plant. Building up a vigorous constitution means conditioning yourself to any kind of weather, and that means plenty of outdoor activity all the year round. It will be the weaklings who worry and fret about the weather, draughts, colds and chills.

Above all else, don't be inactive, a sitter and a lounger. Beat this inactivity and you can be sure your heart will be much stronger and you will feel more energetic and full of vitality.

PART II

Exercises

Getting-up Exercises

The feeling you have when you arise in the morning is perhaps the best index of your fitness. If you wake with a sluggish physical condition you know you are not fit, and you must reorganize your daily routine with rest and work periods and develop good eating habits. Never, never go to bed on a full stomach. Have something light; an orange or a health drink will do.

Never force yourself to exercise. You must develop a mental approach to exercise, and once you have this, together with sensible living, you will start the habit of getting in good condition.

Two bowel movements each day will be most healthful to fitness. Establish a habit of evacuating the bowel at regular morning and evening hours. Don't be discouraged if you are not successful at first. Habits are formed only through repetition.

Exercise One

While still in bed and above the sheets, stretching at full length is splendid for general purposes. Lie flat on your back, stretch legs down towards the foot of the bed and stretch arms up to the head of the bed as far as they can reach. Bend arms if necessary. Arch your back and lift your chest, breathing in to fill the lungs. At the same time make your abdomen as flat as possible. Try it again, then, while reaching down with one foot, raise other knee up to your chest. Clasp your hands over the knee and press it up a little further by pulling it to your chest. Try the same thing with the other knee. Repeat ten times.

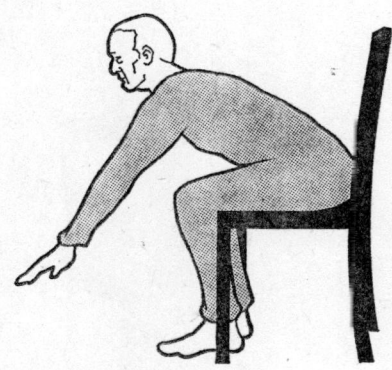

Exercise Two

You have a chair in your room, or possibly a stool or a dressing bench. Perhaps you have never thought you could exercise while sitting down? Just sit well back in the chair with head held high, chest well raised and body erect. With feet together in a natural position bring knees together also, then raise your arms in front of you to the height of your shoulders. Bend forward and reach for the floor. Exhale as you bend forwards, inhale as you come to the upright sitting position. Repeat ten times.

Exercise Three

Sit erect in the chair, slowly inhale and count one, two, three, four, as you place your hands behind your neck. Hold your breath, slowly bend forward and keep your elbows back and your head high while you count. Sit erect again while counting four, still holding your breath. Then lower arms and exhale as you slowly count four. Repeat three times.

Exercise Four

Now sit down on your chair. Sit as straight as possible
with hips and back against the back of the chair. Raise
your arms sideways to the height of your shoulders.
Bring your feet and knees together. Bend sideways from
your hips and try to touch the floor with the fingers of
your left hand. If it is difficult to touch the floor bend
down as far as you can. Do not strain. Return to the
sitting position and then try the same movement on
the right side. You will find that keeping the knees
together will make this a much more difficult exercise
than if you keep them apart. Repeat the exercise about
five times on each side.

Super Lung Breathing

Many people suffer from poor circulation – all because they do not get sufficient oxygen to give a steady blood-flow. The more oxygen you get into the system, the more normal the circulation. When you fill the lungs with oxygen you burn poisons that can cause you harm. Oxygen is in fact a food for the body, and it is vital in purifying the blood. Remember, all the blood in the body passes through the lungs every three-quarters of a minute, and then is purified and enriched by the oxygen we breathe. The lungs are a spongy mass of porous tissue consisting of about six hundred million tiny cells, surrounded by little blood-vessels known as capillaries. The oxygen breathed into the air-cells passes through the delicate lining of the cells and mixes with the blood, which gives off in exchange its waste products known as carbon-dioxide.

I want you to start the day by deep breathing and exhaling. This will only take a few minutes of your time every day. Every morning you should lie on top of the bedclothes. Then, with your legs straight and arms at your side, start a slow inhale until your arms are behind your head. Hold the deep breath for a few seconds. Now exhale and return arms to their former position.

Repeat thirty times and each time try to take in more air, lifting the diaphragm as high as you can.

This movement will also help to strengthen the stomach muscles, as the exercise aids you to get control of the muscles in the stomach region.

Exercise One

Stand erect with feet apart, hands and arms high above your head. Now slowly bend forward, exhaling at the same time, until your hands are touching your feet. If you are unable to touch your feet with straight legs bend your knees a little. Now, from the bent-forward position raise your arms above your head, but do not inhale until your arms are high above your head. Then exhale as hard as you can. Repeat this exercise five times.

Exercise Two

Stand erect, feet together. Now take a full deep breath. When your lungs are full, bend to the left and try and stretch your fingers to your knees. Hold your breath for a count of eight seconds. Exhale and return to erect position. Now perform the same exercise from the right side. Repeat ten times each side. This exercise gets oxygen into the little-used cells at the apex of the lungs.

Exercise Three

Posture breathing. Stand with toes and heels together. Now raise hands overhead. See how high you can lift your chest, drawing in your abdomen. Stretch and stretch and try to touch the ceiling. Repeat exercise eight times. Inhale as you stretch, raise arms above head, exhale as arms are lowering. This exercise also helps to strengthen the muscles that control the erect posture of the body.

Now make it a daily habit to perform these wonderful deep-breathing routines. You will soon have that feeling of well-being, and know the joy of being alive. You will no longer feel fatigued at the least physical effort. There will be a sparkle in your eyes and you will feel mentally alert.

Honestly, isn't it worth a little of your time every day to feel that way?

Home Exercise is Best

Currently there is an admirable drive in Britain to provide more sporting and recreational facilities. They are
badly needed at a time when pressures are more exacting yet leisure time is increasing. However, if there are
no such facilities or gyms near where you live, exercise
presents no problems. Training and gyms naturally
seem to go together, but over recent years top results
have been recognized as coming from home exercise.

This is not to say that I do not encourage gyms and
training centres. In fact if you go with friends, like yourself seeking fitness and health, a competitive atmosphere
can be a good thing. But to my mind home exercise is
all important, and in fact the training programme outlined in this book is designed to be practised using
plenty of home-made equipment at little or no cost.
The advantages are that at home you can exercise when
you wish and adopt a system and routine. This is
especially the case with the housewives and women
naturally anxious to retain their youth, figures and
beauty. These are among the most zealous and determined and, as a result, successful in the quest for good
health.

So forget your age, forget your symptoms and concentrate on getting fit in your own home. At home you can plan the time of your workout, call in a friend if you wish and exercise together. Thirty minutes is all you need to get firm and tuned-up, improving fitness at the same time. Honestly, after only a few weeks you will feel better and look better, with vitality to spare. Have a rest-day between workouts – Monday, Wednesday, Friday would be ideal.

You will need the following home equipment for your keep-fit exercises – a broomstick, three rolled-up telephone directories, a large book weighing about 4-lbs, an electric iron, and a chair.

Now to prepare your barbell. Push the broom-handle through the rolled-up telephone books, leaving room for your hands to hold the broom-handle. To perform the dumb-bell exercise take two of the telephone books off the barbell.

Always remember to breathe correctly during the exercises, so that you fill the entire lungs with oxygen. And exhale as hard as you can. It's a fact that the most active people are those who use the lungs to their fullest capacity.

Take the correct posture positions when carrying out the exercises, and do not rush from one to the next. Perform each exercise slowly and think about the movement and what it is doing for you.

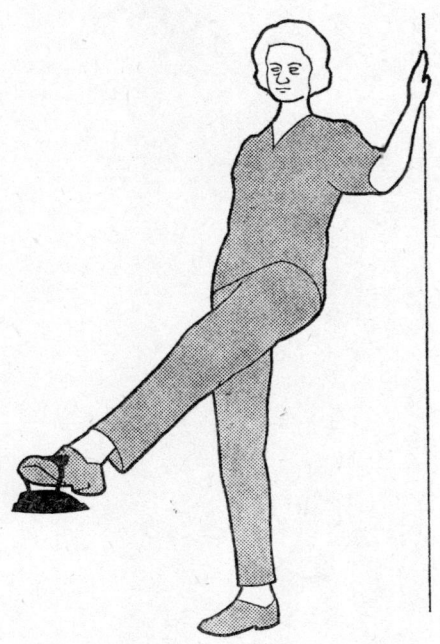

Exercise One

Tie an iron to your foot and, holding onto something,
kick as high as you can without bending your knee.
This exercise is good for the legs and chest because it
promotes deep natural breathing. Swing each leg backwards and forwards fifteen times.

D

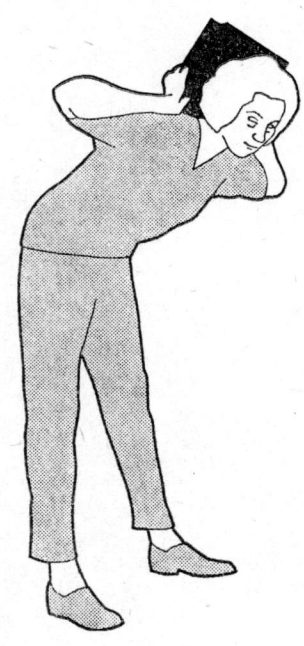

Exercise Two

From an erect position, holding a book behind your head, bend forward as in the picture. Do not lean forward any more than in the sketch. This exercise straightens the back, corrects bad posture, and reduces flesh around the thighs and buttocks. Repeat thirty times.

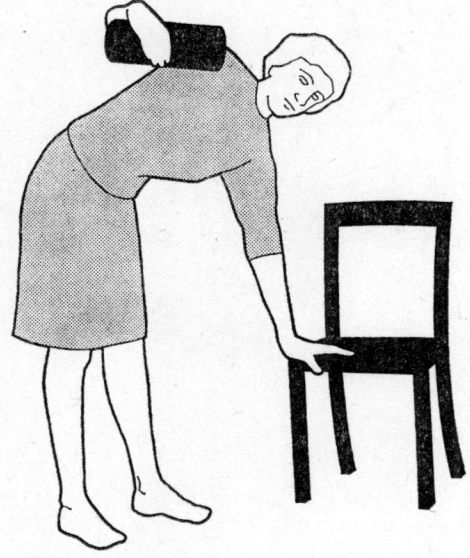

Exercise Three

Hold the rolled-up directory as in the sketch and 'pull' it up as high as you can, inhaling as you do so. Repeat twenty-five times with each arm, supporting yourself on a chair with the other hand.

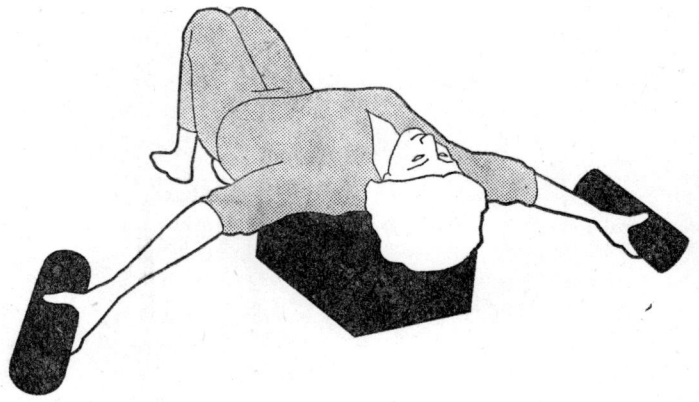

Exercise Four

Get into the position illustrated, holding a rolled-up
telephone directory in each hand. Take a deep breath
and exhale during the actual movement. Bring hands
towards each other keeping arms straight. When your
hands meet over your face – with arms fully extended –
lower them again to the starting position. Inhale while
lowering arms. This exercise helps to form a full firm
bust.

Exercise Five

Hold a book behind you and raise your arms as high
as you can. Then straighten. This exercise helps tone
up a sagging bust. Repeat twenty-five times.

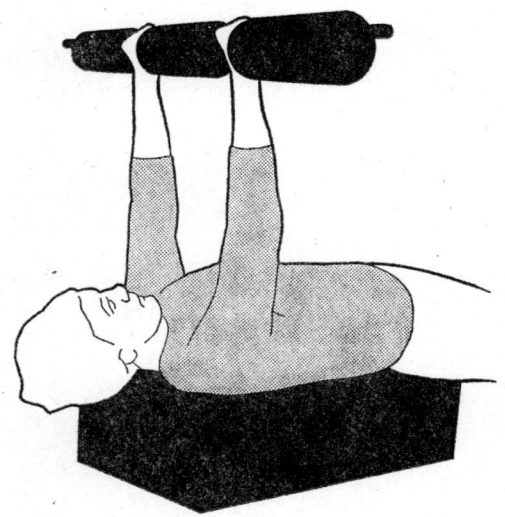

Exercise Six

Lie on a form or box and hold a broomstick with
directories over your head. Bend your elbows and
lower the stick, then press upwards again. Inhale as
you lower the weight, exhale as you raise it. Repeat
thirty-six times, resting after each twelve.

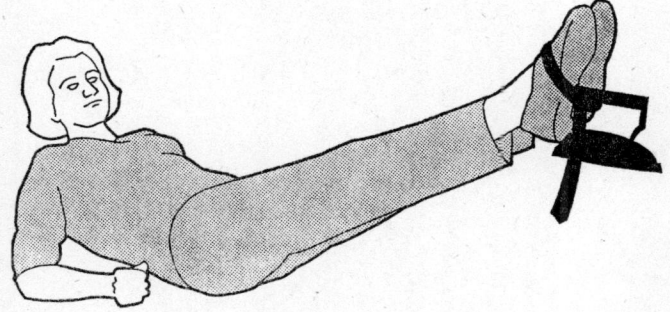

Exercise Seven

Sit on the floor and recline on your hands, forearms and elbows, with a weight strapped to your feet. Hold this position throughout the movement. Take a deep breath and lift legs up as high as possible. Do not bend knees. Return legs to the floor and repeat. This exercise is for reducing the legs and stomach. Do this eight times, rest and repeat eight times more.

Exercise Eight

Stand straight, legs as shown in sketch. Hold a weight,
such as an iron, at arm's length over your head in both
hands. Then bend as far right and as far left as possible.
Make this one continuous movement with rhythm.
Repeat ten times each side, then rest and repeat ten
times more.

Bill Watson's classes exercise in concert.

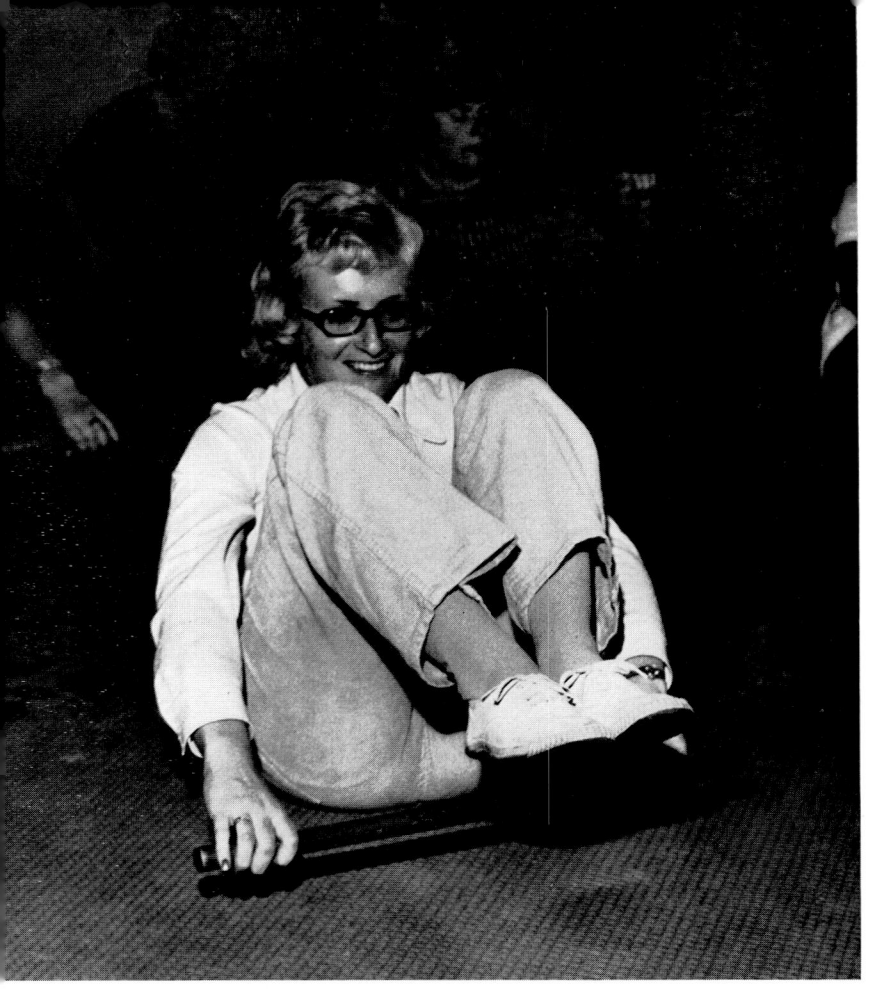

One of Bill's pupils concentrates as she carries out simple
exercises to the best of her ability.

All age groups work side-by-side in an exercise to firm up the
mid-section.

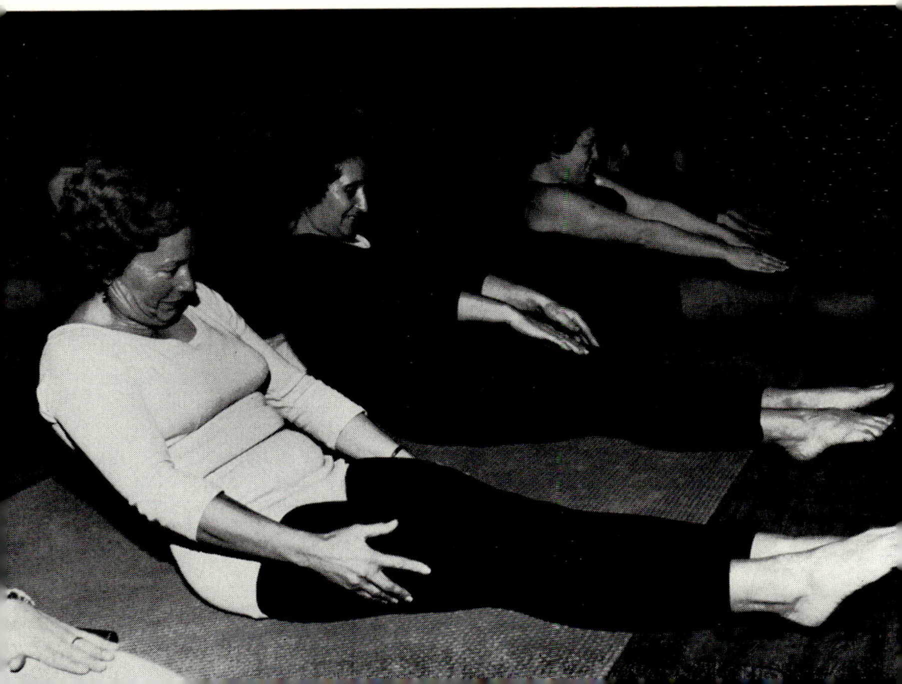

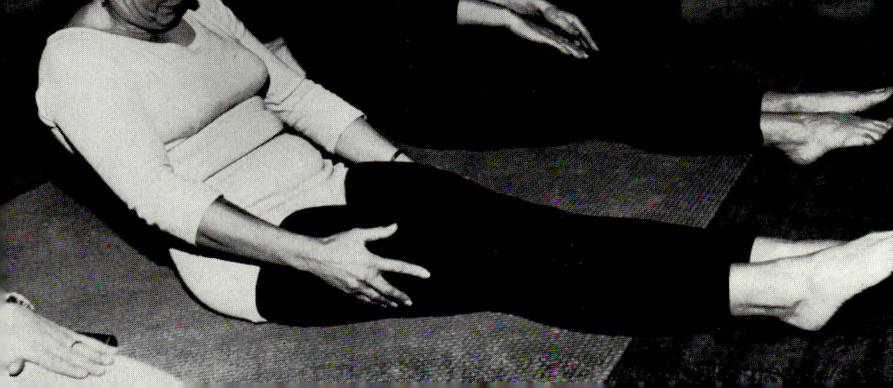

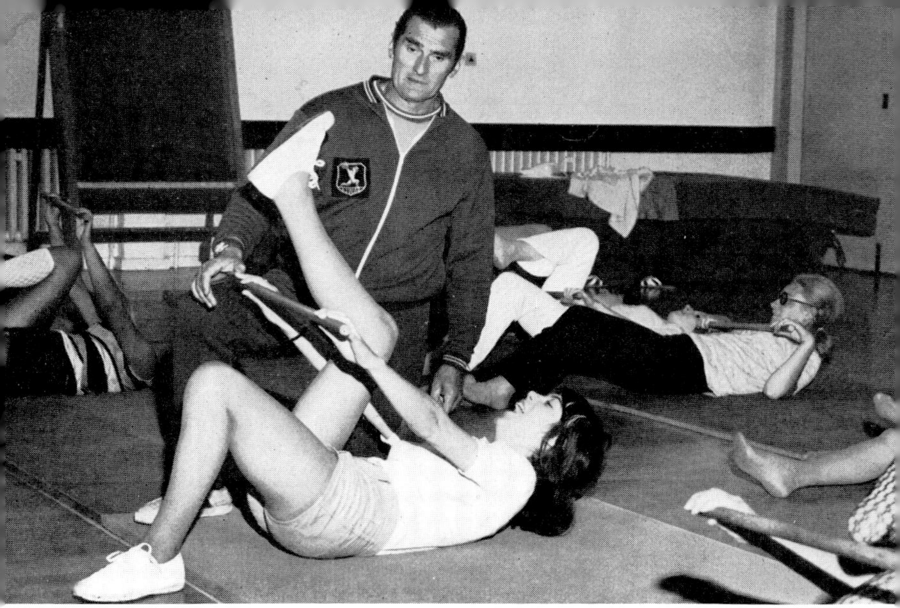

Bill Watson supervises a younger pupil in one of his classes.

Victor Sylvester and William Rushton with L. Murray at a London West End gym.

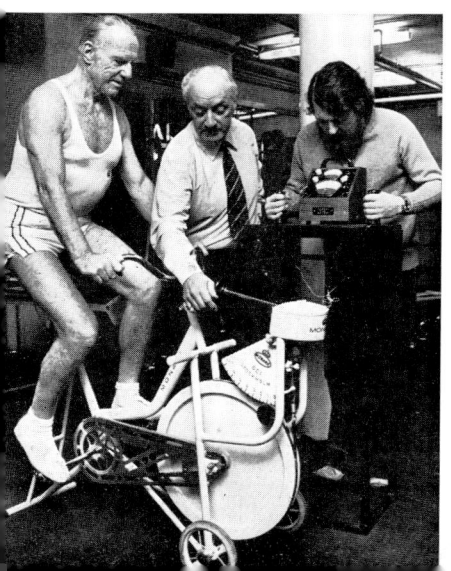

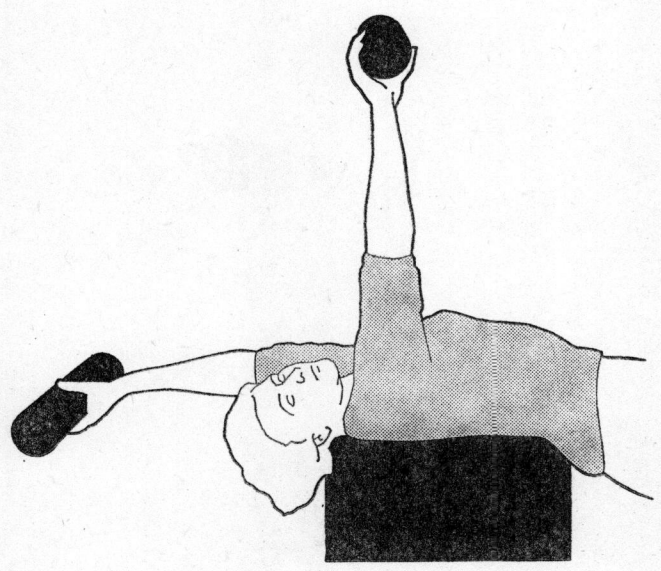

Exercise Nine

Lie on a bench, or suitcase, or box, with your head hanging over the edge, and hold a rolled-up directory in each hand. Hold the books alternately over your head, lowering the other arm behind your head. Do not bend arms. Repeat ten times with each arm.

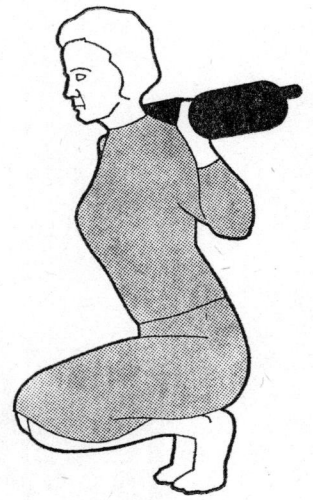

Exercise Ten

Squat down, holding the weighted broomstick as in the sketch. Raise yourself to a standing position, inhaling as you do so. Exhale, and before bending again inhale and exhale five times. Repeat twenty times. This exercise increases lung and leg power.

Remedial Exercises

In this chapter, I am dealing with everyday problems such as flat chests, weak ankles, weak wrists, thin arms, double chins, undeveloped shoulders, dropped stomachs, poor posture, cramp, poor circulation, round shoulders, and thin, weak necks. All these defects respond to exercise and a good healthy diet, always providing the right exercise is used. Of course, progress is slower at forty and over, but, make no mistake, improvement can be made.

I have also found in many cases that exercise helps in cases of digestive troubles, constipation, muscular rheumatism, and poor stamina. None of these defects require drugs, which in effect weaken the very function you want to remedy. You can come to rely more and more on medicines from the doctor and chemists, and eventually the condition can become chronic. If you have any of these problems I want you to take yourself in hand, and following nature's way, embark on a serious system of physical training.

First, let me show you how to strengthen weak feet. I know something about this from personal experience, because, as you will remember, I recovered from badly-damaged feet during the war when they were crushed between an Army truck and a brick wall. As a result, I was told I would never walk properly again, but I was determined to recover from my accident with specially-devised exercises.

STRENGTHENING THE FEET

To be performed twice a day, morning and night. Rise up and down upon your toes, with toes resting on a thick book. Return heels to the floor each time before lifting and stretching them as high as you can. Vary the exercise sometimes by turning feet inward. Perform four sets of twenty movements.

WEAK ANKLES

Again a fairly thick book is needed. Stand astride the book with the sides of your feet resting on the book. Now lift and turn your ankles inward until your knees touch. The outsides of your feet should be well off the floor. Return the outsides of your feet to the floor and repeat thirty times. Rest sixty seconds, then repeat thirty times. Carry out this exercise twice a day, morning and night.

STRENGTHENING THE GRIP

The forearm muscles play a great part in exercising the fingers – the stronger the forearm the stronger the fingers. Carry in your pocket a small rubber ball. Grip it hard and hold the grip as long as possible before letting go. Repeat the action on and off as many times in the day as you can.

FLAT CHESTS

Lie on the floor with your shoulders resting on a low box or cushion. Hold a pair of heavy books as dumb-bells. Now hold the books overhead so that you are looking up at them. Now circle the books over your head and alongside your body and back up again until they are overhead at the starting position. Repeat this exercise twenty times for five sets, resting thirty seconds between each set. Remember that arms must remain straight throughout the movement. Inhale as arms circle over head. Exhale as arms return to starting position.

WEAK WRISTS

Hold a broom-handle at its exact centre. The head must be left on. Now with your arm straight out in front of your body, twist your wrist from left to right. Let the handle turn wrist round as far as possible before turning wrist the other way. Repeat ten times to the right and ten times to the left. Repeat the exercise with other hand for the same number of movements.

CRAMPS

One of the reasons for some types of cramp is the inability to throw off the accumulation of acids and wastes in the tissue created by exercises. It is possible that the circulation may be somewhat impaired, which impedes the elimination of the waste materials located in the area. It is always wise to consult your doctor and discuss the trouble with him. Perhaps you need additional calcium and vitamin C to supplement your present diet. You can obtain these vitamins from the health-shop.

You should avoid cramp by not overworking the areas where you suffer most. When you do experience cramp take a hot bath and soak for at least fifteen minutes.

UNDEVELOPED SHOULDERS

To develop the shoulders you must work on the deltoids, the big round muscle at each end of the shoulders. At forty and, indeed, well over fifty, you can stimulate the shoulder muscles, and, of course, it's a much slower process than when a younger person is concerned, but improvement can be made. Most shoulder exercises also bring the chest muscles into action, so that not only do the shoulders improve but the chest, lungs and breathing also benefit.

I have devised two exercises for you to carry out daily.

Exercise One

Take up a seated position holding two heavy books. For a man the books should weigh about 5-lbs each, and for a woman about 3-lbs each. Now slowly raise arms until they touch overhead, slowly lower to your sides, and repeat fifteen times. Repeat four sets of fifteen movements, inhale as arms raise, exhale as arms lower.

Exercise Two

Take up a lying position on a bench. Now hold the books overhead and slowly lower to your sides as far as they will go so that you get a full stretch of the chest muscles. Exhale and return arms to overhead position. Inhale as arms are lowered again. Repeat twenty times, rest sixty seconds, and repeat four sets of twenty movements.

POOR CIRCULATION

Poor circulation is caused by lack of exercise and insufficient oxygen. Remember the body is made up of a series of pipes, and if you allow these pipes to become clogged you begin to shut off the life-force. To have a pure clean blood-stream you must have oxygen, which is the greatest of all earthly purifiers.

The body must also be fed the correct foods, such as fruits, vegetables, carrots, beetroots, celery, cabbage, turnips and radishes. Leave out of your diet heavy acid meats. Give up alcohol and tobacco and all fried foods. Instead, bake and grill your meats.

Now for the exercise: Stand erect with feet together and arms at sides. Now jump astride and at the same time raise arms above head and hit hands together. You should inhale as arms are raised and as hands hit together try to hold the inhale for two or three seconds. Return arms to sides and at the same time exhale. Repeat ten times, building up the movements until you reach twenty. Take your time with the jump, resting for at least three seconds between. Watch how your vitality and breathing will improve after only a few weeks – but you must carry out this exercise every day to obtain the fullest lung capacity.

THIN ARMS

Thin arms are a problem with many people. This is something that can often be overcome with exercise, and I have been successful in building and adding bodyweight to men's and women's arms when they were well into their fifties.

You will require a broom-handle and two pails, one at each end of the handle. Add sand or earth to the pails. You must find out how much poundage you require yourself. Now hold the broom-handle about one shoulder-width apart at the hang position, with the handle resting on your thighs. Now slowly curl upwards. Palms of the hand should be turned upward. When the handle touches your chest, slowly lower to hang position again. Repeat ten times, rest sixty seconds, repeat four sets of ten movements and carry out daily. Inhale as you bend arms to chest, exhale as you straighten arms. As the weeks go by you will notice your arms getting stronger and fuller and it is now time to increase the poundage. Don't overdo the sand or earth. Add a little once a week.

WEAK NECK

A strong neck may one day save your life. When the muscles of the neck are strong there is less chance of injury to the cervical (neck) spine when the head is whipped about in car accidents or falls.

Strong, thick muscles of the neck provide built-in protection against cutting or penetrating injuries that might otherwise sever blood-vessels or nerves. Head-aches sometimes occur as a result of a weak neck, as every vein and artery passes through the neck to the head. There are several good exercises to strengthen the neck but the one I want you to perform is perhaps the best one to suit you all.

All you need is a fairly long towel and some sort of weight weighing about 4-lbs. An old flat-iron would do the trick. Now loop the towel around your head and fix it firmly. At the loose end of the towel tie on the flat-iron. This end of the towel should be hanging in front of your face. Now bend forward and place your hands on your knees. With your trunk now bent well forward, lower your head as far down as you can and then slowly lift it as high as you can. Try and perform a full range of movement – that is, lower head until chin is touching chest, and lift head until chin is pointing as high as possible. Repeat twenty times daily. Breathe in your own time.

DROPPED STOMACH

Bad posture is one of the reasons for a dropped stomach, so before you embark on an exercise programme to tone up the stomach, take note of your posture. Sit and stand correctly. Carry your head high, lift up your chest, tuck in your behind and draw in your tummy. Then hold this position for two minutes while you walk around the room.

Now for the exercise to help you tighten up the whole of the mid-section. Place feet on a chair with your back flat on the floor. Now swing arms forward from behind your head and touch knees with your hands. Your trunk will then be off the floor. Return trunk to the floor at the same time return to starting position. Exhale as you sit up, inhale as you lie back. Repeat five times for four sets of five movements. Repeat daily.

E

WEAK FLABBY WAIST

The most effective way to trim and firm the waistline is to practice exercises that directly involve the muscles of the mid-section. Of course you cannot have a slim waistline if you are overweight and flabby.

Once you are down to your correct body-weight with a good health diet, and at the same time working hard at a waist-toning exercise, you will see the mid-section as you always wanted to see it – firm, slim and hard. Remember, too, that you can still firm up the waist well into your fifties. The most effective exercise is the sit-up twist, and you must perform this daily. With your feet on a chair and your trunk on the floor, sit up, and at the same time swing your arms from behind your head and touch your right foot with your left hand. Drop back to floor and sit up again and this time touch your left foot with your right hand. This time swing your left arm well behind your body. Repeat five movements to each foot alternately. Exhale as you sit up. Your feet should be held firmly by a partner. Repeat four sets of five movements. Exhale as you sit up, inhale as you lower back.

DOUBLE CHIN

One of the best exercises for correcting a double chin, firming and toning the muscles under the chin, is to move the head forwards and backwards from a lying position with your head over the edge of a bench while holding a small weight or dumb-bell on the forehead. Now lower your head as far back as you can, holding the weight in place with your hands. Your hands are only to balance the weight. Repeat the exercise twenty times daily. Breathe in your own time.

FACIAL EXERCISES

Facial exercises can be done at any time of the day, either in the morning or evening. To stimulate circulation, and to help firm away wrinkles, here are three exercises you can carry out for several minutes at a time to tone up the face muscles and firm the cheeks.

Exercise One

First suck in cheeks sharply and then relax. Repeat for a full minute.

Exercise Two

Stick out your tongue as far as you can and at the same time open your eyes as wide as you can. Hold this position for ten seconds at a time for one minute. This movement will help to tone the skin around the eyes, and will also help to firm up chin tissue and avoid wrinkles.

Exercise Three

Blow out your cheeks as hard as you can and hold the position for ten seconds at a time for one minute. This facial exercise will also help to soften rigid set lines and give the face muscle tone.

These three exercises will bring the blood to the face area, and stimulate circulation and at the same time improve your complexion.

Overcoming Backache

The exercises in this routine are spine motion exercises. A flexible spine keeps you young. The spine is not just one long cervical bone, but a flexible column with a great number of small bones called vertebrae. Each pair of vertebrae is separated from the next by a soft cushion of cartilage. The spine also houses the spinal cord, which passes through the large central cavity formed by the many pairs of tiny bones. The nerves also pass through the openings between the bones. If the spine begins to lose flexibility and mobility, there is a settling of the spine or shortening, and there is less space between the spinal bones. As the bones come closer together they crowd those nerves to the point where they come in actual contact with the vertebrae, causing pressure and sometimes pain. You can counteract this by stretching the spine out to almost its former correct length.

A total of 50,000 people a day are likely to be off work with some kind of back-trouble. I believe that a lot of these back injuries are caused through bad posture when sitting, driving a car, and lifting. The first need is for a strong flexible spine with the muscles firm and strong. You just cannot feel well and full of life if your back and spine are weak. I have illustrated three very effective exercises to help you overcome a weak back. They are easy to carry out at any time of the day. Remember, don't miss a day. And remember too that a healthy back keeps you youthful and full of life.

If you just cannot bring yourself to exercise at home, I suggest you join a keep-fit class. I run ladies' classes sometimes with as many as seventy in a class, and the ages vary from sixteen to seventy-five. Some people work better when exercising in groups and with an expert coach giving sound advice.

Never say you are too old to exercise. I hear this all the time and it is just not true. Such excuses are really just a way out for the lazy person.

You do not have to put up with backache. In many cases it is not necessary. Get the back and spine working again. The muscles of the back should at all times be strong, firm and supple, and you should be able to touch your toes with legs straight without strain.

We, in this country, should take a leaf out of the Japanese book. For a long time they have realised to the full the beneficial effect of keeping fit, and they now allow their office and factory workers time off daily for gymnastic classes. This is always with the consent of the management, as they know that physically-fit workers boost production by cutting down illness which would otherwise keep them away. This of course makes real sense when you think about it. Coronary attacks are now known to be associated with jobs involving prolonged sitting positions. Afters hours of sitting in one place, you may have to sit even more while you drive home, and then at home the evening may be spent sitting and watching television after a heavy meal.

No wonder we have back troubles, stiff necks, stiff joints, stomach complaints, tension headaches and heart troubles. Let's start right away and develop the fitness habit.

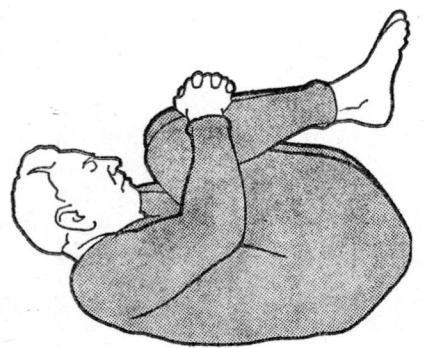

Exercise One

Lie on the floor on your back, hands at sides. Bring knees to chest position, clasping arms a few inches below knees. Now pull knees and thighs tightly against chest. At the same time raise your head and try to touch your chin to your knees. Hold this squeezing position at least five seconds. Return legs to straight-out position. Repeat ten times. Exhale as knees bend to chin, inhale as legs straighten. Carry out daily.

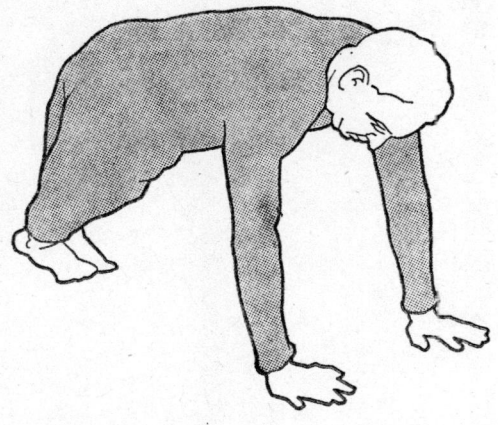

Exercise Two

After a moment's rest from the first exercise, with face down, resting on hands and toes, the back arched, you swing your pelvis from one side to the other – to the very limit of your ability in each movement to the right or left. This, too, should be done slowly. Take time to do it right. Think always of the s-t-r-e-t-c-h we must give the spine. Repeat five times each way and carry this exercise out every day.

You will find the motion tiring at first. It never should become perfectly easy for it is more than a simple swaying your body must have – you must make every one of the long row of vertebrae pull away from the one next to it.

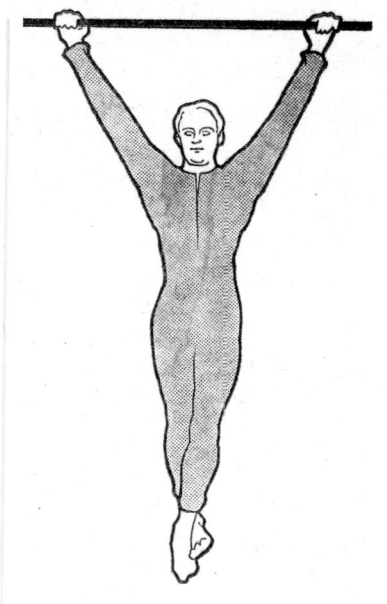

Exercise Three

Hanging from a bar is perhaps the best back exercise of all and takes up little time. Just hang from the bar and try and become as limp as possible. First cross your left leg over your right, and then your right leg over your left. Hang for twenty seconds every day, until you are hanging for fifty seconds. This exercise will stretch the spine from the neck to the base of the spine.

Improve your Fitness for Golf

Golf today is probably the game which is advancing most rapidly in popularity both from the playing and from the watching angle. The top-line professionals and the many big-money tournaments they play in have received growing television coverage over recent years – and this has all helped to activate increasing participation in the sport, especially from middle-aged men (and women) and retired people too. Golf, in fact, is a wonderful sport for healthy exercise. There is a considerable amount of walking involved and there is the clean fresh air to breathe. It can be heartily recommended as a wonderful relaxation, away from the pressures of everyday living. Perhaps this is why there are many middle-aged businessmen to be seen up and down the courses of the country.

What one must remember is that weight-training and the right sort of exercise can be of tremendous help to the average golfer. All the top professionals – Tony Jacklin of Great Britain, Arnold Palmer, Lee Trevino, and Jack Nicklaus of America – weight-train in preparation for their arduous professional careers.

At the amateur level it is an unfortunate fact that in

winter and spring, while golf-clubs gather dust, the players' muscles also suffer through inactivity. Indeed, a winter's programme of training should really be retained all the year round since it not only helps golfers keep in shape out of season, but also provides the strength and stamina needed for the playing campaign.

Experts stress that one of the most important physical attributes for golf is strong legs. It has been said a golfer's legs are the basis for everything: balance, position and consistency. The case of the famous American Sam Snead – now well over sixty – underlines this point. A well-known golf pro and coach, Bob Whitham of Santa Rosa, California, once said of Snead, 'You can tell by the way he walks, he has a fabulous pair of legs.'

Strong legs provide the golfer with a firm position for the swing, while the arms and hands generate most of the power. Strong forearms and flexible wrists play their part here.

Certainly, I advocate golf as a splendid sport for the healthy over-forty man and woman. Have you ever considered the walking involved? I reckon that, on average, with an eighteen-hole course, it could amount to around four miles for each round played.

Many of my pupils are golfers, and they have quickly found that a systematic course of weight-training exercises will always improve their golfing ability. Working out twice a week with weights, the first improvement noticed is that several yards are added to the drive. Balance, stamina, flexibility, speed, timing and concentration are also helped to a marked degree.

Exercise One

Wrist-strengthening. You will need a rolling-pin and a

strong piece of string secured around the middle of the rolling-pin. Now with a 5-lb weight hanging from thirty-six inches of string slowly roll the weight up with the overhang grip. Repeat this movement five times.

Exercise Two

Dumb-bell presses to strengthen shoulders. Hold the dumb-bells at shoulder level. Now press dumb-bells over head alternately ten times with each arm. Dumb-bells should not be more than 10-lbs each to start with. Repeat two sets of ten each arm. Inhale as you press weight over head.

Exercise Three

Squats with barbell to strengthen legs. Hold a barbell across the shoulders, of not more than 30-lbs to start with. Now, with feet sixteen inches apart lower the body into a squat, aiming to keep your heels flat on the floor with your back flat and straight. Repeat for two sets of ten movements. Exhale as you squat. Inhale as you straighten.

Exercise Four

Curling with barbell to strengthen arms. Hold a barbell of not more than 10-lbs, to start with across your thighs. Now, with your body erect, slowly curl the weight to your chest. Repeat the exercise ten times. Repeat for two sets of fifteen movements. Inhale as arms bend. Exhale as arms lower.

Exercise Five

Pullovers with barbell to strengthen chest. Lie flat on the floor with 10-lb barbell on straight arms over your face. Now slowly lower weight to floor behind head. Slowly raise to over-face position and repeat fifteen times. Repeat for two sets of fifteen movements. Inhale as weight is lowered to floor. Exhale as weight is returned to over-face position.

Exercise Six

Straight-legged dead lift with barbell to strengthen lower back. Stand erect with feet together. Now holding barbell in front of thighs slowly lower weight to floor without bending knees. Slowly straighten to erect position and repeat fifteen times. Exhale as you bend forward. Inhale as you straighten up. When you feel ready to increase the weight only do so by 5-lbs.

Light Dumb-bell Training

When you are over forty, fifty or even seventy, you will still want to retain some of the muscular development of your youth. We all know that muscles become flabby and soft, and will virtually waste away without a certain amount of exercise, but exercise is essential to maintain general good health as well. Arthritis and hardening of the arteries often occur through lack of exercise and over-eating, which overload the stomach and other organs of the alimentary canal. The heart, also, can become soft and its muscle-power less effective.

Exercise, on the other hand, will promote efficient circulation of the blood and, although it is possible to overdo this, the normal fatigue that follows regular and reasonable use of the muscular system is a healthy sign. Thus, exercise not only gives the body a feeling of well-being, but also ensures that all the organs function normally. But, of course, unaccustomed or violent exercise should always be avoided.

However, in order to retain our youth we must aim to keep the entire muscular system functioning effectively. Remember that the skeletal framework of the body is both motivated and held together by muscles and ligaments, and other vital organs are also sustained and supported in the same way. Remember this, and keep active so that the body is able continually to reject the dead cells which both cause and indicate the ageing process.

LIGHT DUMB-BELL TRAINING FOR MEN

Exercise One

Forward rowing for arms and back. Maintain a bent-forward position with a dumb-bell in each hand. Pull the bells up to chest and slowly lower to the starting position. Inhale as the dumb-bells are raised and exhale as they are lowered fifteen times.

Exercise Two

Alternate dumb-bell curl, for biceps and forearms.
Alternately curl the dumb-bells from a position at the
sides until they are brought to the shoulder. Inhale
when bending arm, exhale when straightening arm.
Ten times each arm.

Exercise Three

Alternate dumb-bell press for triceps and shoulders.
Hold the dumb-bells at shoulder-level. While breathing
in, press the right one to arm's length overhead. As you
return the right dumb-bell press the left one up. Continue in this see-saw fashion until you **have** done an
equal number of repeats with both arms. Ten times
each arm.

F

Exercise Four

Wide leg-squats for thighs. With hands on hips lower
trunk to full squat position. Exhale as you bend, inhale
as you return to standing position. Twenty times.

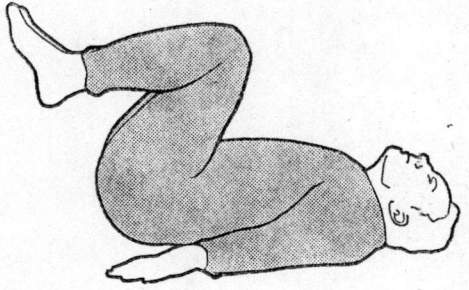

Exercise Five

Leg-bends for thighs and mid-section. Start with knees bent. Then slowly straighten legs. Bend knees again slowly. Repeat ten times, exhale as knees bend, inhale as knees straighten.

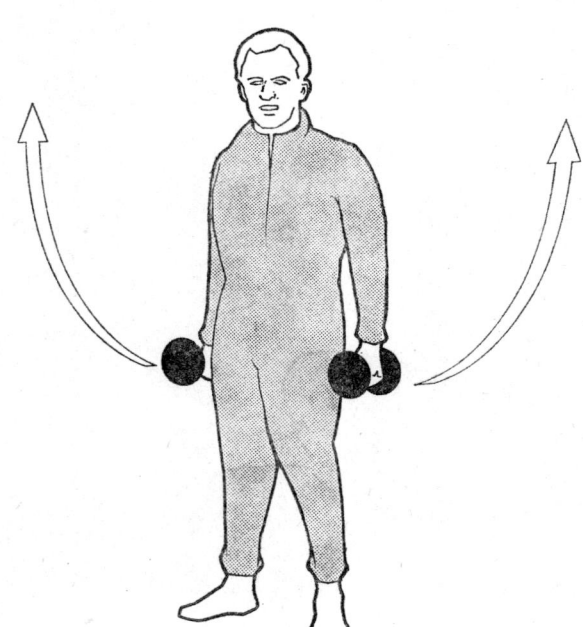

Exercise Six

Shoulder-swings. Inhale and raise dumb-bells to shoulder level. Exhale and lower dumb-bells to legs. Repeat ten times.

Exercise Seven

Forward-bends. Hold one dumb-bell over head on
straight arms. Then, with legs wide apart, swing dumb-
bell down and touch right foot. Return to overhead
position and swing down to left foot. Repeat seven
times each foot. Exhale as you bend, inhale as you
straighten. My dumb-bells weigh 10-lbs each.

LIGHT DUMB-BELL TRAINING FOR WOMEN

When you first start this course begin slowly, giving yourself plenty of time to perform each exercise. Rest between each new exercise. If you wish to concentrate on one problem only at a time, carry out one of the four exercise plans before moving on to the next plan. When you have finished the course start all over again. You might only be interested in a general tone-up and keeping fit. In this case select two exercises from each plan and do them several times daily. Carry out this plan faithfully and you will see a wonderful improvement in posture – a firm and feminine look to the bust-line and a more shapely figure. If you cannot afford the added expense of buying dumb-bells, just tightly roll together two heavy magazines. You will then have a perfectly good pair of dumb-bells at approximately the required weight of 4-lbs. each.

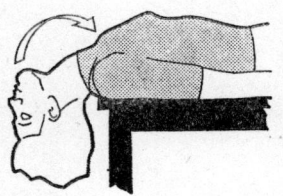 

Exercise One

To firm and tone chin and neck muscles. Lie on a table with head hanging over the edge. Now slowly let head drop back as far as you can. Now raise head and try to touch chin to your chest. Repeat ten times. Now twist head from left to right slowly. Carry out twenty movements in all.

A Four-Exercise Plan to Shape and Slim the Hips and Waistline

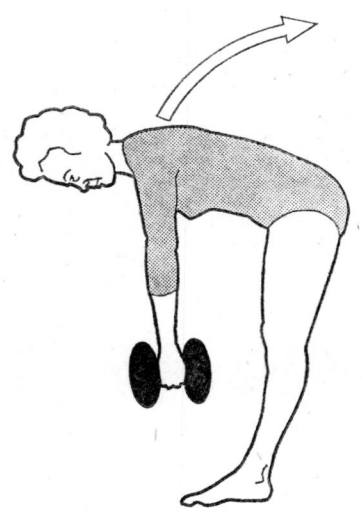

Exercise One

Hold two dumb-bells from the hang position. Now bend forward and touch your toes. Regain upright position and repeat twenty times. Exhale as you bend, inhale as you stand upright. Perform with straight legs.

Exercise Two

Take up squat position shown in sketch. Now, holding on to the back of the chair, stand upright. Repeat fifteen times. Exhale as you squat, inhale as you stand upright.

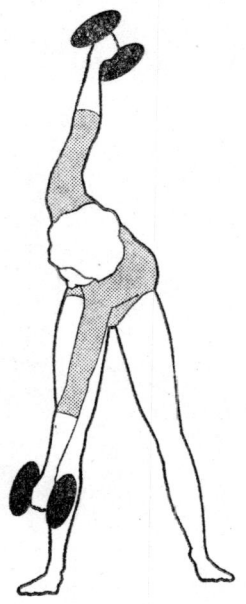

Exercise Three

Stand with feet astride and dumb-bells hanging at the thigh position. Swing right dumb-bell overhead on straight arm and, at the same time, swing left dumb-bell to foot on straight arm. Repeat ten times alternately. Exhale as dumb-bells reach toes.

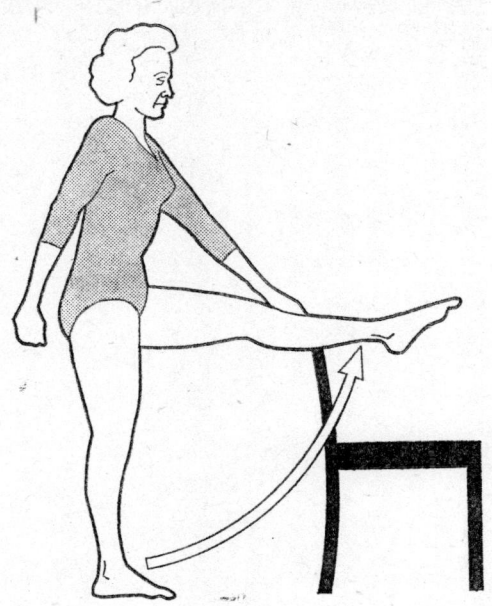

Exercise Four

Take up position shown in sketch. Now with left hand
holding the chair back swing left leg over to hand.
Perform ten times with left leg, ten times with right leg.
The legs must remain straight. Hold the chair with the
right hand to swing right leg.

To whittle and streamline your waist and hips, perform these exercises twice daily. I personally recommend a morning and evening session.

A Four-Exercise Plan to Trim and Slim Abdomen and Buttocks

Exercise One

Take up position as in the sketch. Now with arms stretched above the head alternately jump and cross legs. To perform correctly stretch the legs as far apart as possible. Perform ten times alternately. Breathing should be in your own time.

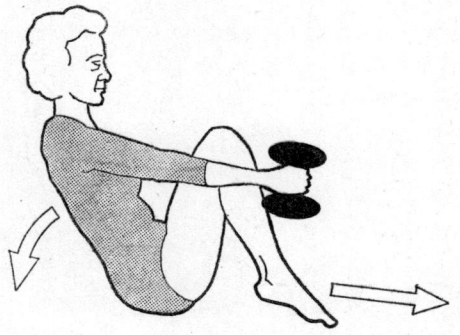

Exercise Two

Lie flat on the floor with dumb-bells beside hips. Now sit up and at the same time draw knees to chest. Repeat fifteen times. Exhale as you sit up, inhale as you lower trunk to floor.

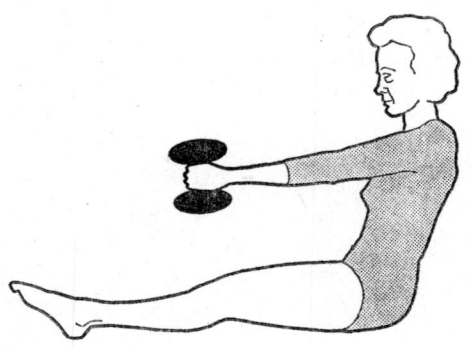

Exercise Three

Take up position illustrated. Hold this position for fifteen seconds. To perform correctly, the dumb-bells must be held in front of chest with arms straight. Breathing should be in your own time.

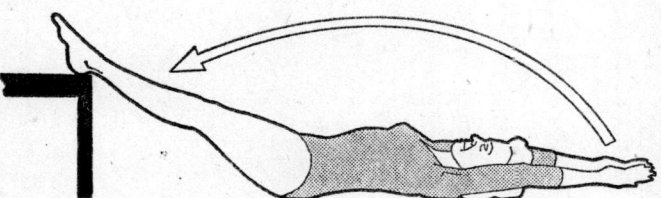

Exercise Four

Place feet on the chair as shown. Now, frcm the lying position swing arms from behind head until hands touch knees. Repeat twelve times. Exhale as you sit up, inhale as you lower trunk to floor. Exercise twice daily – a morning and afternoon session.

A Four-Exercise Plan for the Bust

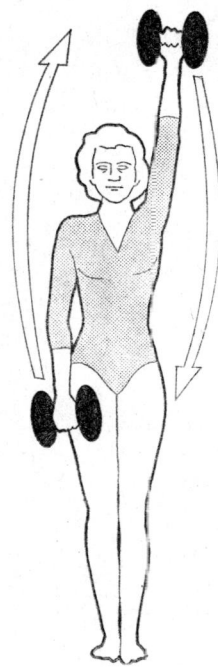

Exercise One

Hold both dumb-bells at hanging position in front of thighs. Swing left dumb-bell overhead. Lower left arm and swing right dumb-bell over. Repeat twenty times alternately in slow time. Inhale deeply as each arm is raised over head.

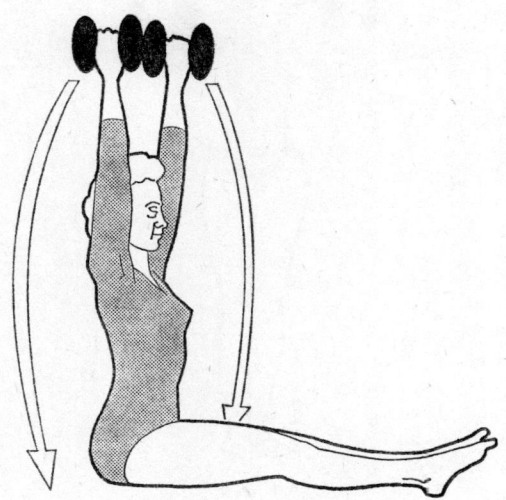

Exercise Two

Sit in position shown in sketch. Lower the dumb-bells outward from overhead position until they touch the floor. With smooth motion raise dumb-bells overhead again. Repeat ten times. Inhale deeply as arms are raised, exhale as arms are lowered.

G

Exercise Three

Take up position with arms crossed as shown. Keeping arms level with shoulders, fling the dumb-bells outwards until arms are in 'scarecrow' position. Return dumb-bells to starting position. Repeat ten times. Inhale deeply as arms swing outward, exhale as arms are crossed.

Exercise Four

Take up position shown in sketch. Holding dumb-bells in bent arm position with elbows held high, swing trunk from left to right. Repeat thirty times.

Perform this routine twice daily. I recommend a morning and afternoon session.

I have two simple rules to help you to a firm bust-line. Stand very straight at all times and sit very straight.

Free Exercise – non-apparatus

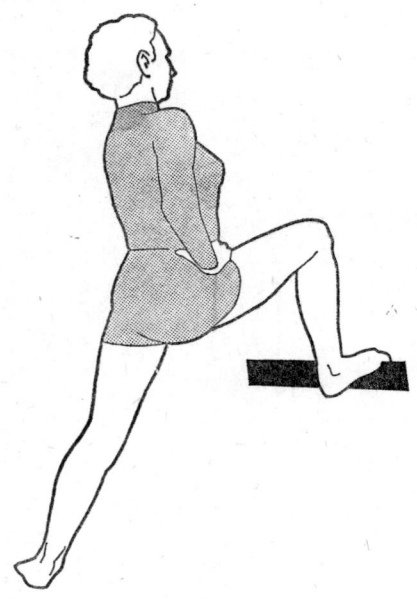

Exercise One

Forward lunge. This movement simulates a step in climbing, so it is very important in limbering up. Place one foot on some object that is about a foot high. Lunge forward and then straighten up again. Finish ten on one leg before changing legs. Eventually work up to thirty twice a day.

Exercise Two

Bend-over stretch. Place your foot on something about hip-high. Start with hands together straight over head. Now bend over and try to touch your toes. Do ten bends the first day and work up to thirty with each leg twice daily.

Exercise Three

Lunge. In this exercise you might wish to hold onto something for balance if you are just a beginner. Otherwise put your hands behind your neck for further resistance to make the exercise more difficult. Lunge forward as shown in the sketch, then bring feet back together. Then lunge forward on opposite leg, alternating back and forth. This is excellent for the entire hip and thigh section of the body. It also works the abdominal muscles, while stretching the upper body if you keep your hands against the back of your neck. It will take you a little time gradually to work up to doing ten lunges on each leg for a total of forty repetitions.

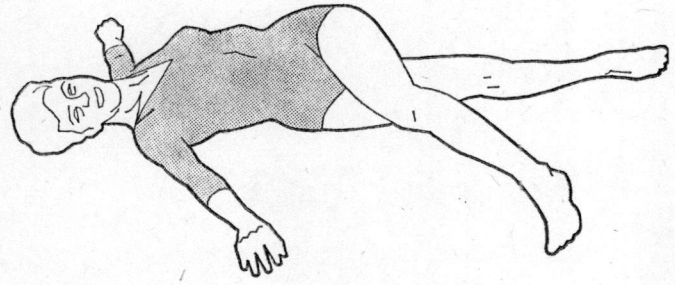

Exercise Four

Leg crossovers for the hips. The sketch shows the crossover. From here the leg is brought back straight beside the other. Go through the repetitions on one side completely, then change to other leg. Ten times each leg. Gradually work up to forty repeats.

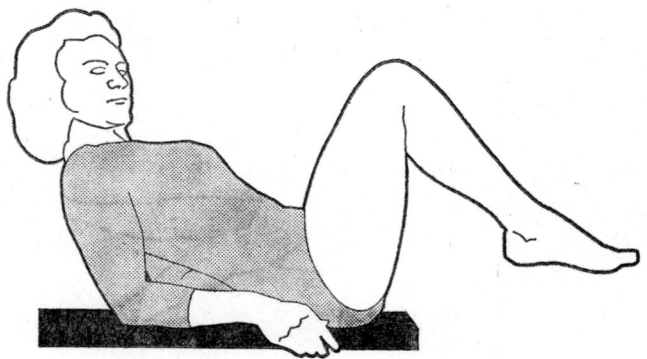

Exercise Five

Recline push-out. Sit on a bench or a firm flat surface.
Lean back and prop yourself on your elbows as shown.
Bring knees up tight toward chest and push out with
medium speed. Keep the action going for at least
twenty repeats. This exercise is primarily for the
abdominal muscles. Inhale while pushing legs forward,
exhale while drawing knees to chest.

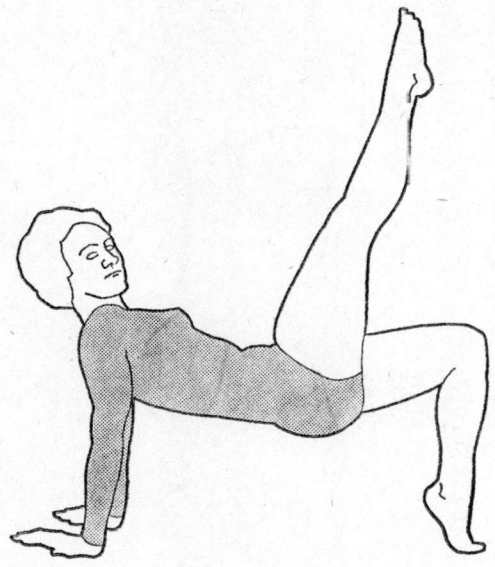

Exercise Six

Straight-body back-kick. While holding onto some
support snap leg back without moving the balance of
body. Tip-toe to the other foot. Perform at least ten
repeats with each leg three times every day.

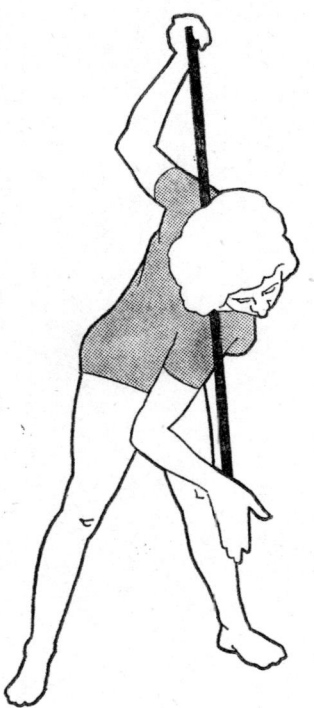

Exercise Seven

Bend-over twist. With a light bar on the back of the shoulders bend over and twist down toward knee as shown. Straighten up, bend over and twist to opposite knee. At least twenty twists to each side three times daily are necessary for the mid-section.

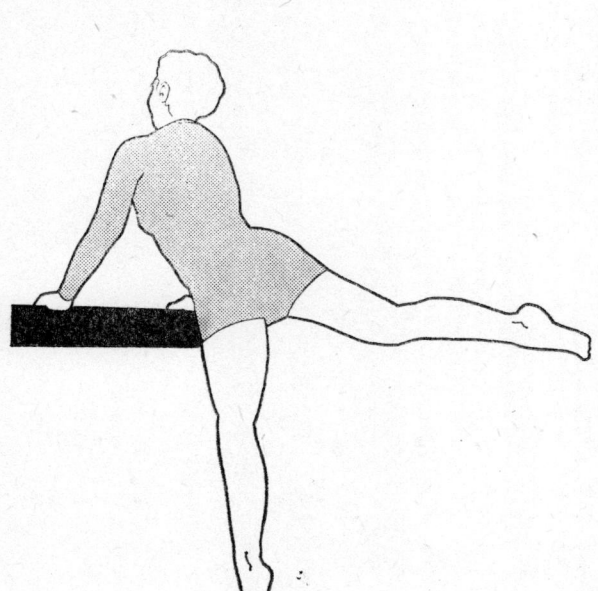

Exercise Eight

Back-kicking. Hold onto something sturdy and rise up on your tip-toes as you kick one leg back smooth, not jerkily. Bring leg back down slowly as you come down off your toes. Do ten repeats and then change to other leg. Work up to twenty back-kicks with each leg by doing two more movements each day.

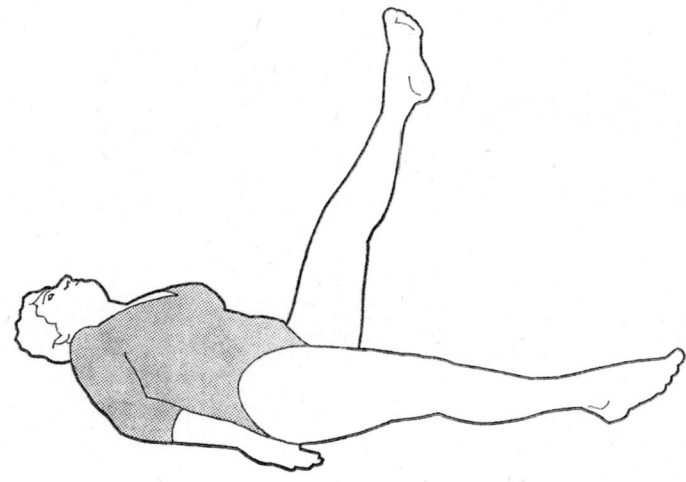

Exercise Nine

Alternate leg-raises to condition the lower abdomen.
Do ten repeats and then change to other leg. Work up
to thirty times on each leg by adding two movements
every day.

Exercise Ten

Perform deep knee-bends with heels resting on a piece
of one inch wood or a thick book. Carry out ten repeats
working up to thirty repeats by adding two movements
every day. Exhale as you squat, inhale as you straighten
up.

This free exercise routine will help to condition and
firm up the whole of the body.

Broom-handle Routine

This is perhaps one of the best exercise fitness-routines I have ever devised. All that is required is a four-foot broom-handle. The movements will quickly improve all-round physical well-being, flexibility, suppleness and stamina. The exercises will firm and slim the waist, and strengthen the arms and shoulders, and the back will also become stronger. In addition, the chest, lungs and heart will be in better condition. Thirty minutes of your time is all that is needed. You can pace yourself through these exercises with at least sixty seconds rest between each. Never at any time rush an exercise. Think about every movement and what it is doing for you. This is the way to improve quickly.

Exercise One

Stand in the upright position with legs as wide apart
as possible. Hold broom-handle above head as shown
in the sketch. Bend to the left and to the right as far as
you can, ten times to the left and ten times to the right.

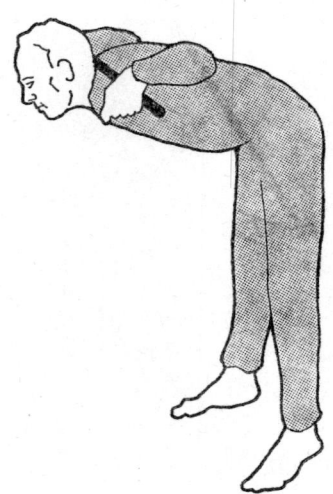

Exercise Two

Hold the broom-handle behind neck. Now bend forward keeping a flat back. Straighten to the upright
position. Repeat this movement forty times. The legs
must remain straight with feet flat on the floor. Perform
as slowly as possible. Inhale as you straighten, exhale
as you bend forward.

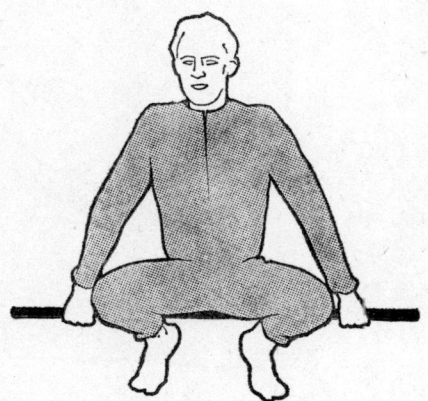

Exercise Three

Stand in the upright position with broom-handle behind thighs. Now, holding a good posture, squat down as shown in sketch. Repeat twenty times. Exhale as you squat, inhale as you return to the upright position.

H

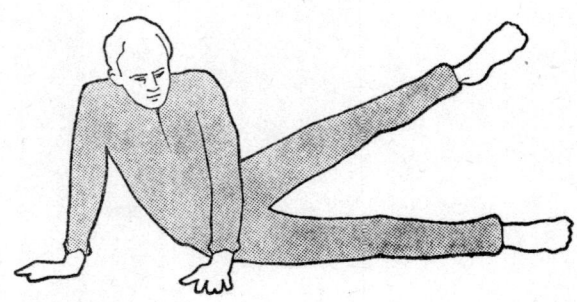

Exercise Four

Take up position as shown. Now raise left leg as high as you can making sure right leg remains on the floor. Repeat ten times with each leg. This exercise will firm up the hips.

Exercise Five

Stand erect with broom-handle held behind neck. Now twist to the right and bend down until the broomstick is as low as possible between legs, as shown. Stand erect again and twist to the left and bend as low as possible until broom-handle is again between legs. Arms and legs must remain straight. Exhale as you bend forward, inhale as you straighten. Repeat twenty times to the right and twenty times to the left. This movement will work the oblique muscles strongly and improve hip-flexibility.

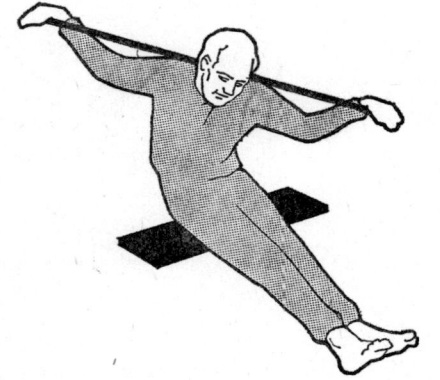

Exercise Six

Sit on a form with the broom-handle across shoulders.
Now with feet together twist trunk from right to left.
Legs must remain straight. Repeat twelve times to the
right and twelve times to the left. This movement will
tighten and firm waist.

Exercise Seven

Stand erect with the broom-handle behind neck. Now raise left leg as high as you can to left hand. Do this eight times, each leg alternately. This exercise will help to slim the thighs and firm the hips.

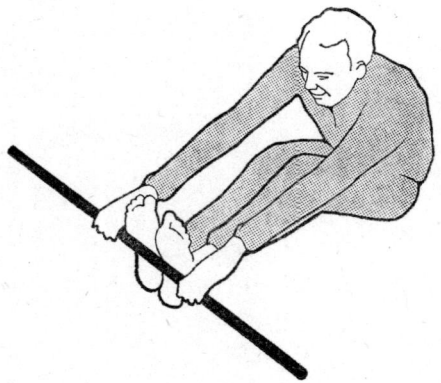

Exercise Eight

Sit on the floor holding broom-handle on thighs. Now exhale and try and reach forward as far as you can towards, or over, the feet. Inhale and return to starting position. Repeat twenty times. In time, you will be able to perform this movement with straight legs.

PART III

How the Stars Keep Fit

Victor Silvester's Way to Health and Fitness

Victor Silvester, the world-renowned ballroom-dancing expert and band-leader, is a truly remarkable man in many ways. He, more than anyone, has brought pleasure to countless thousands through the medium of the modern dance. But besides that, Vic can still bring you plenty of health-giving exercise tips too. Of all the many show-business personalities of television and radio who attach so much importance to keeping fit, he is probably the most extraordinary. It is hard to believe that he is as old as he is; in fact he is a wonderful example to men and women half his age.

Vic has kindly allowed me to use his daily training-schedules for this book. You would do well to study them and follow his lead. He has called them eight simple exercises to bring back and retain youthful vigour. The exercises are intended mainly to develop and retain a full range of movement in all your joints. Breathing throughout should be regular and rhythmic. The exercises from One to Six should be repeated, in full, thirty times on each exercise, number Seven should be repeated, in full, three times at first and then working up to ten times. For number Eight, running on the spot, start jogging for one minute's duration working up to five minutes or even longer.

Bill Watson.

The author performing press-ups. This movement strengthens the arms, chest and shoulders.

The author performing flexibility exercises which keep the body loose and supple.

Bill Watson performs a variety of vigorous movements as part of his own keep-fit routine.

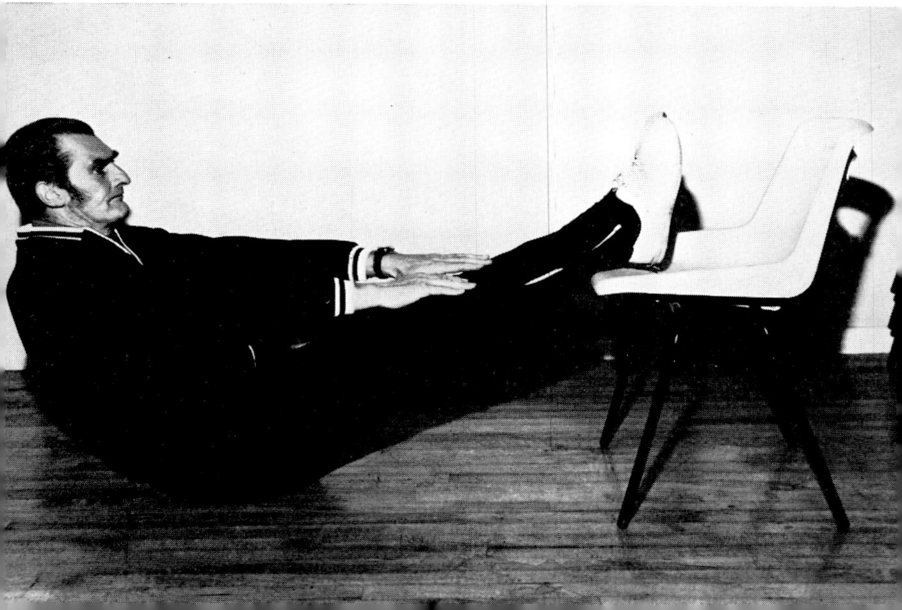

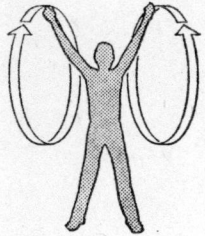

Exercise One

Feet wide astride, arms circling (forwards, upwards and backwards). A continuous circling movement. Stop at thigh on lowering. In three movements.

Exercise Two

Feet wide astride, trunk bending from side to side, hands on hips.

Exercise Three

Feet together, thighs raised to chest, alternate knees.

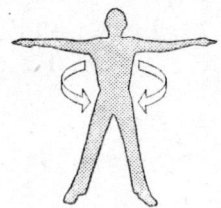

Exercise Four

Feet wide astride, arms sideways stretch, trunk rotating.

Exercise Five

Feet wide astride with arms straight, touch opposite ankle.

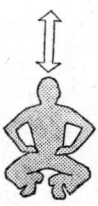

Exercise Six

Full knee-bending on toes.

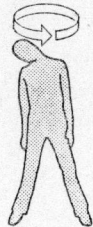

Exercise Seven

Head-circling: rotate head five times one way, then five times the other. Repeat.

Exercise Eight

Jogging, light running on the spot.

When you become really proficient after three to four months' training, endeavour to repeat the entire schedule from start to finish without a pause. This will work wonders for your heart and lungs.

Victor also has a special weight-training exercise-schedule which is very interesting. Working non-stop, the schedule is completed in twenty-five minutes.

Exercise One

High pulls to chin level, rising on toes. Stop at thigh on lowering in three movements. The poundage is 40-lbs bar and repeats are twenty to twenty-five, one or two sets. Victor adds that the pulse is 134 on completion.

Exercise Two

Bench-press. Bar 60-lbs and eighteen to thirty-five repeats, two sets.

Exercise Three

Abdominals, knees to chest, sit-ups. One set of ten.

Exercise Four

Inclined flying. Dumb-bells 20-lbs each. Eighteen to twenty-five repeats, two sets.

Exercise Five

Power-cleans. Lift to chest, stop at thigh on lowering. In three movements. Dumb-bells 20-lbs each. Eighteen to thirty repeats, one set. (Pulse 140 on completion, V.S.)

Exercise Six

Pulley. Pull down to rear of shoulders. Twenty to thirty repeats, two sets.

Exercise Seven

Trunk-bending forwards, keep back rounded throughout. Bar 20-lbs, fifteen repeats, three sets.

Exercise Eight

Running on spot (jogging). Run for five minutes (pulse 120 on completion, V.S.)

Exercise Nine

Breathing pullovers, bar 20-lbs, twenty repeats.

Stars of Stage and Screen

You would be surprised at the number of top-line film stars and television and radio personalities who take a great deal of time and trouble over keeping fit. In their exacting professional life they have to be in peak physical condition. And the big thing, too, is that they enjoy it all.

Running close to Victor Silvester as a keep-fit exponent is that popular disc-jockey Jimmy Young, who in the past few years has shot right to the top as a radio personality. What keeps Jimmy young, you might ask? Well, it was a number of years ago – in the 1950's, to be precise – that he turned to weight-training, about the time that he made a top-selling hit parade number called *Man from Laramie*. Jimmy has come a long way since then, but he has kept up his training-schedule. Jimmy, in fact, has always been an athlete (he was a PT instructor in the RAF) but he had never before turned to weights. He took up a programme composed of dumb-bell swing, swing-bell curl, alternate press, straight-arm pull-over, rowing side-bend and overhead-roll and lateral-raise. For squats he was advised to use a barbell.

Inside eight weeks Jimmy was amazed at his progress. 'I'm really glad I tried this weight-training stuff,' he said, 'it's worked wonders with me. I feel fitter, happier and stronger in every way.' After his eight-week course Jimmy gained 5-lbs in weight, half an inch on his neck measurement, three inches on his chest, one inch on his upper arm, one inch on his thigh, and half an inch on his calf. Jimmy Young has never departed from weights since.

He had never been lazy when it came to sport and athletic pursuits. As a schoolboy he was a champion boxer, and he once sparred with Freddie Mills and Len Harvey. Both these boxers spoke highly of his prowess in the ring. Freddie Mills once declared that Jimmy had real potential and should have turned professional.

Jimmy preferred to make his name in the musical and disc-jockey world. But this keep-fit enthusiast has always been sporting-minded. When in the RAF he taught unarmed combat and boxing.

The immediate success of his weight-training programme delighted him. In fact several of his friends said at the time that he was just as pleased about his bodybuilding as about the sales of those early records, one of which grossed £250 000 at music-shops throughout the country.

'In just two months I put on a solid ten inches of muscle,' he said. 'I got new stamina and confidence that even years of sporting activity didn't give me – and I doubled my strength in that short time.'

Jimmy thought that his golf improved when he took up weight-training. At first, stiff and sore muscles put him off his game a little, but then improved control and increased co-ordination combined to bring about a marked improvement. And of course Jimmy's added energy from weight-training helps him through his busy, hectic professional career.

'I don't want to sound like an advertisement for some patent medicine, but it really is great stuff, this weight-training,' he chuckles.

Another star, of television this time, who follows a keep-fit pattern is song-and-dance man Roy Castle. His dance-routines, as you know, are really something, and Roy feels it essential to be in peak condition at all times. He says: 'I'm not fanatical, but I watch my weight and eat accordingly. I enjoy a good race-about to open the lungs and my act keeps me fairly agile. I always try to sit fairly upright when driving the car and avoid slouching over the wheel. This keeps the stomach muscles tight.' He adds: 'I have been known to go for a five-mile run if work is not too demanding. My motto is – all things in moderation.'

In the world of films, one of the fittest stars of them all is Roger Moore, the new James Bond. His success as the latest actor to play James Bond has been extra-ordinary, and the film *Live and Let Die* has been a fantastic box-office hit.

To match the image of the all-action character of Bond, a star would have to be very fit indeed. Roger certainly makes sure that he is. Weight-training plays a big part in his condition-routines to keep a firm and strong body. Roger, whose popularity reached great heights when he played 'The Saint' in the television series, goes regularly to a London gym. When you see him training you realise the hard work that goes into keeping him in tip-top shape. To survive as James Bond you must be one hundred per cent fit.

Television comedian and the idol of millions of watchers, Dick Emery is another who took up weight-training and sticks to it regularly now. He is in an exacting profession involving much travelling as he fulfills engagements up and down the country. Dick, in fact, carries all his weights, barbell and dumb-bell with him, in a Hertz van.

So many of these keep-fit stars visit the gym of my old friend Ruben Martin that I must give him a special mention. Ruben is now in his fifties and still performs his wonderful strong-man act all over the world with his attractive wife. The pair are known as the De Milles, and their specialist act includes comedy and feats of balance and strength. They have appeared in all the top London hotels, toured Germany, Italy and Holland, and been on television in shows like *David Nixon's Magic Box*, *Crackerjack* and the *Rolf Harris Show*. They display marvellous fitness and skill in that fast, tough Apache-type act of theirs that has been featured in television commercials and special French Night shows.

I have known Ruben now for many years. I first met him when we both weight-lifted in the world championship together, and since then we have often competed against each other. I am still amazed at his remarkable fitness and peak condition.

Another star who is a wonderful example for all those attempting weights and planned exercise is the famous singer and entertainer Frankie Vaughan. He is often asked why he spends so much time training with footballers, and going out running himself.

His answer, pure and simple, is always the same: 'I use up so much energy in my stage act that it is absolutely essential I keep in peak condition.' Frankie not only has a busy, action-crammed life in the world of show business, travels extensively, and spends much time in notable charity work, but he also finds the

I

extra time to play football and box regularly. He is a fine example of physical fitness, and in fact he has been nicknamed 'The Body' as a result of weight-training.

The famous American film stars and radio personalities also believe very strongly in keeping fit. Kirk Douglas, that fine actor and star of so many action adventure films demanding fitness and an athletic approach, is one. Kirk certainly does not look his age, and claims that this is due to following health- and fitness-routines.

Then there is Clint Walker, star of so many popular Westerns. He became world famous as the star of *Cheyenne* and he is an ardent bodybuilder, and health-addict. He uses dumb-bells and barbells in his training and always makes a special point of eating the right sort of foods. He has a fine singing voice, the development of which has been attributed to deep-breathing exercises with weights.

A most remarkable lady is charming Katie Boyle. She is now forty-four and looks a stunning thirty-four or less. She stresses that it is very important to look after yourself: 'When I was twenty I laid the foundations for my forties by diet and exercise. Today I weigh 8 stone 12 lbs and still practise yoga exercises. I do not smoke, or drink and always eat the correct foods. Every Sunday I diet by drinking only four glasses of hot water with pure lemon and a teaspoon of honey in each. The good foods I love to eat are leafy vegetables, salads, onions, tomatoes, citrus fruits, berries, eggs, steamed or roast meat, fish and poultry. I exclude pork, herrings, sardines and goose.' She is really a wonderful advertisement to us all.

Even stars who do not weight-train follow exercise-routines. Fred Astaire, world-famous as one of the greatest dancers of all times, Gene Kelly who followed him in that world and the apparently ageless Cary Grant, are prime examples of what exercise can do.

Of the numerous female film and television stars, probably the most remarkable of all is Hollywood's Mae West, who captivated audiences in the cinema of the 1930's. She is another ageless marvel, who still trains every day with 15 lb dumb-bells and is a firm believer in deep-breathing. Her skin is still remarkably youthful.

In this country no woman personality has commanded more attention with her keep-fit ideals than the attractive and effervescent Jill Day. She has her own gymnasium at her home, equipped with barbells and dumb-bells. Her weight-routines have aided her perfect figure and she is also very strong, swinging across a rope with the ease of a lithe cat. Jill's training has helped to sculpture her body. Many people wrongly think that weight-training will build big bulging muscles. This has been proved incorrect beyond all doubt. Weight-training, specially designed for women, is one of the best ways of moulding a shapely and attractive figure. Following Jill Day's example television singer Ruby Murray, who also has a fine figure, has been weight-training for a number of years and now, with her husband, she operates her own keep-fit gym.

Older Personalities

Age is of course no barrier to health and fitness. For example, there is that remarkable old man of Somerset, Ernie Underwood. He is over eighty. And in the 1914–18 War he lost a leg at Ypres! This astonishing man is still trying to break his own weight-lifting record, established way back in 1934 when he set up the 'British ten-stone lateral-raise lying'. Ernie has never lost this record. His secret, apart from weight-exercises, is an intake of plenty of prunes, milk and honey. Every morning he is out in the garden on the horizontal-bar he keeps there. Then it's muscle-building exercises and that special diet.

On the subject of remarkable old men, we should mention the late George Bernard Shaw. It is not generally known that the famous author and playwright had his own ideas on exercise and fitness. When he died he was well over ninety and tremendously fit and active for his age.

Shaw the intellectual, the wit, the notable playwright, played an active game of golf when he was sixty; there are photographs of him at seventy baring his chest and yelling a Tarzan war cry. Even at eighty he dug, and chopped logs, and at ninety he was still a good walker. Shaw was always a champion of physical fitness. In his early days he scoffed at specialised exercise and went on record that he thought he could get as much benefit from digging the garden. But later he changed his mind, adding with characteristic dryness that when a person reached his age they were entitled to change their opinions at least once! I don't think anyone should dismiss Shaw as a crank, and his ideas about fitness are certainly worth reflecting on today.

'I like to think I'm strong rather than big,' he once said. 'Do you think I would be better off if I had a fifty inch chest and weighed five stone more? Would I want to carry about all that surplus weight at my age?'

Shaw, who in his youth had carried out cable exercises, admitted in later years that he thought they laid the foundation of the physical fitness that lasted him all his long life. He believed in sport of all kinds and was of the opinion that the stomach muscles and the small of the back were the two main centres of health.

'What gives out first when you have a real job of work to do?' he said. 'The back, of course. And what is acknowledged to be man's weakest part? The stomach; attend to these two parts and the rest will take care of itself.'

Shaw was convinced that a sound mind in a healthy body is what everyone should aspire to achieve. One day he said: 'I will write a play on bodybuilding and put it all down.' Alas, he never did, but there is no doubt that this wonderful old man might have lived even longer had he not been the victim of an unfortunate accident.

One cannot finish this chapter without a final word about the leading fitness and health expert in the United States. Paul Bragg, a nutritional physical fitness exponent, and his daughter Patricia, have a systematic programme of exercise, deep-breathing, sunbathing and natural hygiene. Paul is coming up for ninety and looks only fifty. He swims, rides, hikes, tackles mountains. Once a year he climbs Mt Whitney, the highest mountain in America apart from Mt McKinley in Alaska. One of his firm beliefs is in mind-power, and he says that before he goes on a long swim or climbs a mountain, he mentally sees himself accomplishing the feat he expects to perform. It seems to work. On one occasion he went on a marathon trek through ninety miles of difficult terrain on a diet only of health food and left far behind exhausted men and youths years younger than himself.

PART IV

Food and Diet

Any diet, to be satisfactory, must include those foods which contain substances to help the body to produce heat and energy, to grow and to be able to repair damaged tissues, to protect the general health and working of the body.

Most normal foods contain one or more of the essential substances in a greater or less proportion.

The necessary nutrients are carbohydrates, to give energy; fats, which do the same; proteins for growth and repair; minerals for growth, repair and control of the body's processes; and vitamins, which also control the way the body functions.

Carbohydrates are found mainly in sugars and starches and no present-day western diet is likely to be deficient in these. Proteins are found in fish, meat, eggs, dairy produce and many other items of everyday food. Cheese and peanuts are excellent sources of protein. Fat, of course, is found in vegetable fats and oils, animal fats and dairy products. The minerals are generally only needed by the body in very small amounts and most normal diets contain an adequate quantity.

The vitamins deserve some individual attention.

Recommended Foods

This vitamin is essential for growth, and a lack of it affects the eyes and the mucous membranes. A daily requirement would be about 750 micrograms, which could be obtained from one ounce of liver.

The carotene in yellow and green plants, fruits and vegetables is converted into vitamin A in the body, and this accounts for about two-thirds of the total amount of vitamin A in the average diet. One ounce of cooked beef liver supplies 1,700 micrograms of the vitamin. Fish-liver oil is the richest source of vitamin A.

Try to get the vitamin A you need from natural foods. Since this vitamin can be stored in the body, an unduly large amount supplied by a synthetic supplement can have toxic effects, and you should be very careful not to take excessive quantities which would cause a poisonous reservoir to accumulate. Remember that vitamin A is a fat-soluble vitamin which is found most abundantly in fatty foods of animal origin. So if you are on a low-fat diet, you might want to consider taking a vitamin A supplement.

VITAMIN D

This vitamin helps to supply the bones with calcium and phosphorus, so it is particularly important for pregnant women, babies and children, although everybody needs a certain amount. Cod liver oil is very rich in vitamin D and so are dairy products. Sunlight also helps to form vitamin D in the body, so if children are in the sunshine, they will need less of the vitamin in their food.

VITAMIN C

Vitamin C strengthens tissue cells by supplying them with a 'cement' that holds them together. It also strengthens the collagen or connective tissue that keeps flesh from sagging. Vitamin C must be present when new cells are formed. Since 98 per cent of the atoms in the body are replaced each year by new atoms from food, air and water, there must be a constant supply of vitamin C. Since your body does not store vitamin C you must have a daily supply.

Fresh fruits and vegetables contain this vitamin. To get the amount you need to prevent colds and delay the ageing process, however, you should probably take a natural supplement that will provide you with an extra supply. It may be better to take three or four small doses rather than one large dose. Too much at a time may force your kidneys to eliminate much of the vitamin.

30 milligrams is considered an adequate daily amount and this can be obtained from one ounce of blackcurrants or a couple of ounces of raw cabbage. Vitamin C is easily destroyed by cooking, however, and green

vegetables can lose more than half of their vitamin C even if they are carefully cooked.

VITAMIN K

This vitamin, which is found in green vegetables, is necessary to help the blood to clot; most people's natural diet contains an adequate amount of it.

THE B VITAMINS

The B vitamins, of which there are several, are essential for growth and health; lack of some elements in the B complex can lead to stomach upsets and even to mental symptoms. Dried brewers' yeast is the richest source of all these vitamins, with liver as another source. Wholemeal bread also supplies some B vitamins, but not a very large quantity, particularly as some is lost in cooking. An ounce of dried brewer's yeast would supply the daily need, but obviously most of the vitamin B will be taken into the body through ordinary foods, such as liver, cheese, eggs and bread.

VITAMIN E

Every cell in your body needs oxygen to keep it alive. Without adequate vitamin E, however, that is, about 750 milligrams oxygen tends to oxidize or destroy the essential fatty solids, forming a peroxide substance that ages tissue-cells and destroys blood-cells. Like a piece of unpainted iron near a sea-shore, body tissues age or 'rust' in the presence of oxygen when there is a deficiency in vitamin E. It is essential for normal metabolism.

Vitamin E also tones the heart muscles, dilates blood-vessels, improves circulation, and prevents the formation of clots in veins and arteries. Even the collagen that holds tissue-cells together needs vitamin E to keep it flexible and healthy, giving it the elasticity of youth. You also need vitamin E to protect vitamin A, which is required for tight, youthful skin. In some cases, the addition of vitamin E to the diet will actually reverse some of the symptoms of premature ageing.

Natural sources of vitamin E are to be found in all types of green leafy vegetables, seeds, nuts, whole-grain cereals and breads. But the best natural sources are wheat-germ and wheat-germ oil. A natural vitamin E supplement can be used to supply additional amounts of vitamin E daily. Always buy natural vitamin E since it is about five times more potent than the synthetic variety. In addition to supplying vitamin E, a teaspoonful of cold pressed-wheat-germ oil each day will supply the essential fatty acids you need for stamina and to combat hardening of the arteries.

IMPROVE CELL FUNCTION WITH CALCIUM

When the body is deficient in calcium, the bones become brittle, nerves cannot function normally, contraction of the heart muscles is disturbed, and the tissue-cells are unable to exchange wastes for nutrients. Calcium deficiency can cause premature ageing. If you take a calcium supplement, remember that you must also have vitamin D, phosphorous, magnesium, and other vitamins and minerals to absorb and utilize the calcium. Milk and milk-products are good sources of calcium. Bone-meal enriched with vitamin D is one of the best sources, since it contains the correct ratio of calcium and phosphorous. You need at least 500 milligrams of calcium each day. Make sure that any supplement you take contains more calcium than phosphorous. An excessive amount of phosphorous (as in an all-meat diet) may force your kidneys to eliminate calcium.

HONEY

Honey has been called the food of the gods, the nectar of life. In medicine it has had remarkable success in alleviating many ills. Certainly it plays a big part in my keep-fit programme for you, alongside milk, which I have already mentioned, and cider vinegar.

Have you ever asked yourself exactly what honey, this magical substance, is? To most people it is a pleasant, sweet stuff collected by bees. But in actual fact there are numerous kinds of honey and they all have different tastes. It is a complex substance which varies from flower to flower and from soil to soil. The composition of the soil upon which the plant is feeding is probably the biggest single factor. And it is affected by climate so that, for example, there will be a difference between the clover honey of Australia and the clover honey of California. Both too will be different in lots of ways from English honey. It has such a wide range of flavours that it can be likened to wines. As there are vintage years for wine so there are for honey – and they usually coincide, for both need hot summers and plenty of sun.

Briefly, honey sets out as a thin water-sugar fluid, called nectar, which is usually sited in the base of flowers. Nectar is the plants' offering to honey-bees in exchange for the service these insects render in pollinating them. Plants differ when it comes to the sugar and water content of the nectar. With the dandelion, for example, the nectar is made up of roughly sixty per cent sugar and forty per cent water. Pear blossom on the other hand has a water content of up to seventy per cent. The substance the bee extracts is a liquid made up of sucrose, rather like cane-sugar, with other ingredients and water. Inside the bee, the nectar is stored in a tiny compartment and various and complex changes then take place. Playing their part in the conversion to honey are enzymes and juices, so that honey consists of the two simple sugars of dextrose and levulose.

More changes occur in the hive or in the hollow of the tree. The liquid will be exposed as a thin film to the warm currents of air in the hive, and thus the water-content is rapidly lost. When no more than about eighteen per cent of the water remains the now ripened honey is sealed in a cell with a waxen cap and left to mature. It is really a fascinating story of nature and one which, if you are interested, is well worth studying in more detail.

But from our health and fitness point of view the complex sugars, acids, minerals and proteins that make up the highly nutritious ingredients of honey are what must be remembered.

One of the outstanding physical properties of honey is its hygroscopicity. In other words it has a great natural attraction for moisture. It is the hygroscopicity of honey that makes it a great healing power. Disease germs in its presence cannot thrive and are quickly destroyed.

Minerals in honey vary widely from one type to another. It is the darker honeys that usually contain the greater amount although, like the vitamin-content, they are relatively small. Loss of minerals in the human body means, of course, a decline in energy and vitality. Honey may not contain any vast quantity o minerals, but when added to a normal diet it does increase the mineral intake, and as such is much better than artificially-produced sugars. The main mineral needs of the body are calcium and phosphorous, followed by potassium, chlorine, sulphur, sodium and magnesium. The body also has a smaller requirement for copper, iodine, iron, manganese, zinc and fluorine. Iron is of vital importance to the blood stream and manganese to the many enzyme systems. It is the primary metal for the enzymes of the citric-acid cycle, the metabolism where most of the final oxidation to carbon-dioxide occurs.

Vitamin-content in honey is small but important. Again it varies in types of honey. The vitamins present are ascribed to pollen-content. The higher the pollen-content the more vitamin value. Some research workers have found that honey is a first-rate medium for vitamin stability, while fruits and vegetables tend to lose much on storage.

Before discussing honey as an aid to medicine, let me say some words about its health and diet uses. Too many people feel it is just for spreading on bread and butter or swallowing as a soothing influence to ease a cough or a cold. Another popular use of honey is sweetening cereals or porridge with it. Mix a little hot water with a small quantity of honey, and it will pour perfectly.

Honey in a jar will begin to cloud if left, and from a bright liquid becomes sugary and often set. This is not at all detrimental to the honey, and the simple solution is to place it in a pan of hot water for a while. Then it will again become liquid.

Another idea is to flavour tea with honey instead of artificial sugar. In this choice, select a mild honey, such as clover or acacia, that is sweet but not strong-tasting. There are a variety of uses for honey as food, in cake-making, and bread-making, for example. Honey-drinks and even a type of honey-beer have been produced. There have been a number of good books published on the subject with plenty of interesting recipes.

The history of honey is an interesting one. It dates back to paleolithic times, when primitive man consumed it in its crudest form. With the advance of the first civilisations the substance became of supreme importance both on medical grounds and in religious observance. Biblical mentions are numerous and the Greeks believed it would prolong life.

No one is pretending of course that honey is a miracle-product, full of supernatural powers, but certainly there is a great deal of evidence of its use to medicine and surgery, going back to antiquity. As a treatment for the dressing of wounds there are countless stories. It is a fact that antiseptic dressings involve the use of strong chemical substances which can to a greater or lesser degree have a poisonous effect in the body-tissue but daily dressings of honey on lint with effective bandages have been found to heal injuries.

There have been cases also of legs ulcerated from varicose veins being aided by regular daily application of honey. And deep flesh wounds, too, especially when the wound may have turned septic, have been healed in this way. During the First World War and the last war, German troops' wounds were treated with honey to good effect. And for sufferers from hay-fever and sinus troubles, it is also beneficial.

One doctor prescribes honey for hay-fever, telling his patients to chew honeycomb cappings once a day for a month before the hay-fever season starts. For mild attacks of hay-fever this should be done once a day or every other day. Should honeycomb not be available, two teaspoonfuls of liquid honey with each meal will give the same results. For sufferers from sinus complaints, coughs and colds, the use of honey can also be recommended. The symptoms of sinusitis are blocked nasal-passages and, frequently, pains at the front of the head. As the membranes that make up the sinuses are very thin, treatment can be difficult.

It is recommended that a sinus-sufferer chews one mouthful of honeycomb four to six times daily. It should be chewed for fifteen minutes or so. Eating honey as part of the general diet can help also.

I recommend too, some other popular remedies. People who suffer from nerves should take a tablespoon of honey diluted in a tumbler of warm water with the juice of half a fresh lemon every day. It helps steady nerves and is good for sleep.

Other suggestions

Bad colds and excessive hoarseness. Peel and chop a pound of onions, to which add two ounces of honey and three quarters of a pound of brown sugar in two pints of water. Then simmer gently over a low heat for three hours. When cool cork the mixture well and take four to six tablespoons daily.

Measles. Raspberry tea and honey is ideal. Take two to three warm cups a day.

Throat and chest complaints. A blend of honey and blackcurrant is good. The mixture should comprise a tablespoon of blackcurrant jam mixed into a quarter of a pint of boiling water. Strain and add two drams of powdered citric acid, three drams tincture of squills and six ounces of liquid honey.

Cough mixtures. Mix six ounces of liquid honey, four ounces of treacle and five fluid ounces of quality vinegar. Simmer over low heat for fifteen minutes and bottle and cork when cold.

Or, mix six ounces of liquid honey with two ounces of glycerine and the juice of two lemons. Mix well and bottle, corking firmly.

Honey and codliver oil emulsion can also be easily made. Add one ounce of glycerine, one ounce of essence of almonds, eight ounces of honey and five fluid ounces of lime-water to eight ounces of good codliver oil. Mix well and cork tightly. This is undoubtedly a good winter standby.

Last, but by no means least, honey has tremendous advantages when it comes to beauty treatment. Its use for women in this respect goes back to early civilisation. It is said indeed that Cleopatra used ointments and balms containing honey and beeswax. And it is a fact that a great deal of honey these days is used in cosmetics. The honey has elements that soften and heal skin-tissue, and its hygroscopic properties attract moisture to the skin.

Beeswax is a staple emulsifying agent, and that explains why most good lipsticks are made with a beeswax base.

K

For women who would like to bring a natural youth-fulness to their skin, a simple facial is recommended. With a third of a cup of finely-ground oatmeal blend three tablespoons of liquid honey. Add a teaspoonful of rose-water. After cleansing the face with water spread the facial mixture evenly and relax quietly for half an hour. Then carefully remove with a soft face-cloth and warm water. Rinse in cold water and then watch for the results. You will find that you will regain a lovely soft skin. The treatment is particularly good for those with oily skins.

A good treatment for chapped or work-roughened hands is the following cold cream, inexpensive and effective. In a pan put six ounces of honey, four and a half ounces of clean beeswax and six ounces of lard. Melt together, remove from the heat and stir until cool. Then add two drams each of attar of bergamot and attar of olives. Also for chapped hands you can take the white of an egg, a teaspoonful of glycerine and one ounce of liquid honey, kneading them to-gether with sufficient barley-flour to produce a paste.

Last, but not least, use honey as a hair-aid – although this treatment is recommended only for brunettes. To four ounces of liquid honey add two ounces of pure olive-oil and then store away in a warm place. Before washing your hair give it a treatment. Shake the bottle so that the honey and oil mix thoroughly. Massage a generous amount into the hair and scalp, working the lotion in for some minutes. With a hair-dryer warm the head and allow the lotion to remain for up to half an hour. Then wash the hair in a good soapy shampoo. There is no guarantee that this treatment will stop hair greying. But without doubt it will assist the hair to keep its colour and healthy lustre and is ideal for the scalp.

Honey is a really marvellous natural health-giving food and aid to medicine and beauty treatment. Never be without it!

MOLASSES

Another health shop necessity, in my view, for those who want to achieve fitness and vitality through my programme, is molasses. Our civilisation today is one of wonder drugs and patent foods. Many of the foods are good in counteracting the effects of a diet that is lacking in vitamins and mineral salts. But several of those wonder drugs tend to have had their day and do more harm than good. Be that as it may, a number of experts have described molasses as nature's wonder food. There is nothing whatever 'patent' about it and it can be bought in most health-food stores and shops. Recently molasses tablets have appeared on the market, but experts state that it is the molasses liquid that plays the major role in its beneficial powers and in this form it is by far the most effective.

Molasses is made up of 39·5 per cent sucrose, 11·5 per cent invert sugar, 9 per cent ash, 22·5 per cent water, and 17·5 organic matter. The percentage of ash represents soluble mineral matter that is largely made up of potassium and calcium salts. When we come to more detailed analysis we find iron, copper and magnesium, and the whole mineral content is a rich source of most types of vitamin B. It is very high in vitamin B6, in pantothenic acid and inesitol.

Another important part of molasses is phosphoric acid. When there is a combined deficiency of this acid, plus potassium in the body a general breakdown of the cells, particularly those of the brain and nerves, can be caused. Crude sugar-cane molasses also contains roughly fifty per cent fruit sugars.

Molasses can and should be used at the table as regularly as salt, taken as a sugar-substitute with cereals, stirred into milk, or used in place of jam and jelly.

There are numerous claims that molasses can cure a number of illnesses, from cancer and arthritis to constipation. While these cannot, I feel, be ignored, it is largely as a health-food and aid to peak fitness that I am interested in this amazing product.

There are so many people today who suffer from what is generally labelled 'nerves', tired feelings, spells of depression, and bouts of neuralgia, 'flu and colds. In fact they keep the waiting-rooms of doctors pretty full all the year round. Gradually, of course, more and more people are taking a good proportion of natural vital foods into their daily diet. Health shops have become more numerous in our towns as a result and the person who uses them is no longer regarded as quite the crank he once was thought to be.

One advantage of molasses is that it can be taken at any time, when it is most convenient, during or after meals. In fact there is no set rule. The dosage suggested is one teaspoonful dissolved in half a cup of hot water, to which cold water should be added to make two-thirds of a cupful. Then it should be drunk warm. The molasses can, if wished, be taken neat, but if so hot water should be drunk directly afterwards. It is really up to the individual, and the individual taste.

The reason for hot water – although it should never be too hot – is that by being diluted this way the

molasses is more easily assimilated and more digestible.
With some people, cold water can chill the stomach.
The water should never be hotter than a temperature
at which you can comfortably bear your finger. If
preferred, you can take molasses in the milk used for
breakfast cereals or porridge. Or it can be mixed with
marmalade and jams made from white sugar.

But there still remains a large section of people who
have rather confused ideas as to what molasses really
is. To many it is just black treacle. The dictionary
definition is 'the thick non-crystallizable dark syrup
which drains from raw sugar during its manufacture;
thickest kind of treacle'. But ordinary black treacle,
fine though it is, is much richer in sugar.

It has been argued that molasses increases the weight
of stoutish people. For these the dosage of molasses
should be lessened, more diluted and taken less frequently. There are complaints also that certain brands
are sweet and sickly. But the correct type for remedial
purposes is certainly not.

No-one pretends, naturally, that molasses is a one
hundred per cent guaranteed cure of cancer and other
diseases, but there have been hundreds of cases of
beneficial effects from a treatment of crude black
molasses, which supplies the body in a natural way with
essential elements. In America there is encouraging
news from certain naturopaths who for some little while
have been treating varicose veins with the molasses
treatment. Likewise arthritis-sufferers have been re-
lieved. Worry, it has been said, is often conducive to
arthritis. Sugarcane molasses is to be preferred to other
kinds, as the type made from better sugar is not so
rich in phosphates.

Claims also that ulcers have been cured are becoming

more prevalent, as well as gratifying reports from sufferers from high blood-pressure, angina pectoris and weak hearts.

High blood-pressure has been linked with a deficiency of certain essential mineral salts. Good results have been obtained by taking molasses with the juice of one lemon a day. The cause of blood-pressure really lies in the arteries losing their elasticity and becoming hardened and blocked so that it is much more difficult for the blood to circulate without considerably increased effort by the heart. An increased amount of the required mineral salts help to keep the arteries elastic, and these salts are to be found in molasses. It also contains other ingredients helpful in strengthening the heart muscles.

Next we come to constipation, a complaint that has rightly been called the bugbear of civilisation. Though I have dealt with this in a separate chapter, I shall stress again that the obvious reason for constipation is that so many people live on deficiency foods and turn to the glut of laxatives on the market.

A great deal of trouble comes from the fact that the bowels have lost tone through lacking the necessary mineral salts. Molasses, which is a mild and natural evacuent, will help in this direction. Crude black molasses is far better than black treacle as an aperient. In severe cases a dessertspoonful or even a tablespoon should be taken in warm water first thing in the morning, plus daily dosages at meal times. Four to six weeks of this treatment is recommended.

It is not surprising when you consider the amount of assimilable iron and calcium in molasses that many cases of anaemia have been helped by it.

In my experience, and considering a wealth of evidence in its favour, there is little doubt that molasses is another of those health shop commodities to which the person wanting peak fitness should definitely turn.

WHEAT-GERM

In addition to the nutritional value and health-giving properties of honey and molasses, I must now add wheat-germ, which is a natural source of vitamin E and other nutritional elements. Wheat-germ is in fact the heart of the grain. It is the embryo from which a new plant may develop. It gives life – and for this very reason, it is claimed by many as a food which will help increase overall health and restore coveted youthful vigour. In the production of white flour the germ is removed, so all products made with white flour are as a result entirely without this essential ingredient.

Health shops have on their shelves wheat-germ oil in bottles and in capsule form and there are also wheat-germ flakes that can be eaten as a cereal. It is suggested that they can be eaten with the addition of dried fruits, chopped nuts or fresh fruit such as apples, bananas or oranges. Honey and milk can also be added.

Health and fitness experts everywhere stress the value of wheat-germ in the diet. It can provide vigorous health, and body-building elements. It is therefore a valuable dietary supplement for those doing hard exercise, and it enables men to bear severe stress without deteriorating. Its special value is in its effect on physical endurance and heart response.

Until wheat-germ oil tests were conducted, vitamin B offered the most encouraging results. But the new product has proved even better. To those outside the field of sport, too, I certainly recommend the inclusion in your diet of this invaluable natural product.

Proper exercise is also very necessary. Physical exercise opens up the blood-vessels of muscles and heart tissues, and increases the blood-flow of arteries, thus allowing the nutrient to reach the muscles and tissue where it is mainly needed.

In America, results in the field of athletics and swimming are certainly worth considering. Even established athletes cannot be kept at a peak of physical fitness indefinitely. Most of them attain a 'high' after about twelve weeks' hard training, and then begin to slump. The American experiments show that with wheat-germ in the diet an even higher peak can be attained. From the University of Illinois ace hurdler Willard Thompson, and swimmer Jody Alderson, both broke records. Before, it had been thought that they lacked the necessary final burst of energy to be top-notch performers.

What worked for them can work for you, in your quest for health and vitality.

REVITALIZE WITH BREWER'S YEAST

Brewer's yeast is one of nature's most nourishing and concentrated foods. In addition to containing vitamins, minerals, protein, and other important food elements, it is rich in nucleic acid, a substance that is present in the life-centre of all living cells. A rich supply of nucleic acid helps keep tissue-cells youthful and healthy so that they can resist the ageing process. Nucleic acid also provides the cell with the framework it needs to give birth to new cells.

Try some brewer's yeast tablets with each meal. The

rich supply of B vitamins they provide will strengthen your nervous system, boost your energy, and help keep hard fat deposits from accumulating in your arteries.

THE MAGIC OF CIDER VINEGAR

It has been said by the world's health experts that pure natural cider vinegar is one of nature's most perfect foods. A really magical keep-fit essential, in fact.

It must be made from fresh crushed apples and then allowed to mature. It is best for the maturing process to take place in wooden barrels. The vinegar should be dark in colour and if held to the light one should observe a formation of cobweb-like substance. Its smell should be heavy and pungent. Generally, cider vinegar is to be found in health-food shops, although some supermarkets have it on their shelves.

The value of the apple is inestimable. The old hackneyed phrase, 'An apple a day keeps the doctor away' is full of truth and sound common sense. We have been apple-eaters since the beginning of time, and apple-eaters have a definite health advantage over non-apple-eaters. The fruit is one of the richest sources of potassium, which is to the soft tissues of the body what calcium is to the bones and the body's harder tissues. It could be termed the mineral of youth.

The apple helps us to stand the test of time, for potassium softens the arteries, keeping them flexible and resilient. It helps fight bacteria and viruses. So, apart from the enjoyment of a delicious fruit, consider the tremendous advantages of eating that apple a day. Many of us are deficient in potassium, and it shows in cell-tissue. How many people have a live-looking skin? Often the skin and muscle tone is bad. This shows in lines and wrinkles and in the flabby skin that droops over the eyes. The longer there is a potassium-deficiency the further this sort of condition will progress. Advancing years, of course, will be blamed for this state. But in actual fact it is potassium that will build youthful tissue.

Look for an example in the garden, where potassium is vital to the production of substances which give rigidity to plant-stems. Potassium is the mineral, indeed, that changes seed into flower by progressive development.

If there is potassium-deficiency the plant will begin to wither, turn yellow and die. And as with plant, so with animal life.

All over the world, even in the 1970's, millions of men, women and children are suffering from many forms of malnutrition. Due to the lack of proper minerals and vitamins they lack vim and vigour and feel tired and listless when carrying out the ordinary tasks of life. What is lacking is the proper amount of minerals and vitamins required. And with the lethargic tiredness comes the frequent use of stimulants like tea, coffee, alcohol and cigarettes. These drugs, as drugs they are, will add temporary pep. But the person's condition will worsen when the effects wear off.

Here are some of the tell-tale signs of potassium lack: aches and pains in the lower back, dizziness when you straighten up after leaning forward, frequently an early headache upon rising in the morning. There is also irritability and impatience, and periods of depression and nervousness.

Certainly, I do urge you all to turn to the magic of cider vinegar and its splendid sources of potassium. Ideally it can be added to pure honey – another natural food rich in potassium. It can be used in salads and, as I will explain, can be taken externally as well as internally.

Cider vinegar will not necessarily cure – but as a fighter of germs and a health-giving mineral it will act as a preventative and assist you in numerous ways. For the overweight person, providing he controls the intake of food, it will help enormously. A vinegar-and-honey cocktail, consisting of half a teaspoon of honey and two teaspoons of cider vinegar in a glass of water can be taken three times daily. Naturally, in addition, there must be the right sort of exercise and diet.

Cider vinegar can also be used successfully by underweight people, since it contains powerful enzymes. The underweight person, is recommended to take, first thing in the morning, two teaspoons of cider vinegar with one heaped teaspoon of honey to one glass of water, plus one drop of Lagos solution. This will provide iodine, which is important in adjusting body-weight.

Many troubles in the body are caused by toxins In several cases we do not have the vital force to supply the eliminative organs with the power to move the normal poisonous waste. The joints and organs of the body become affected, and it is here that cider vinegar can render certain toxic wastes harmless. Recommended for body purification is six ounces of tomato-juice added to two teaspoons of natural cider vinegar. Take this between meals once or twice a day.

The headache is a frustrating, uncomfortable ailment for so many people today. There is, of course, the chronic headache which can often be linked with long-standing disease. This type of headache is really a message and warning signal from nature. But by far the most common headache is the emotional kind brought about by anxiety, stress, strain, tension or any emotional upset.

Many experts think that headaches are emotional in origin, because the urine becomes alkaline rather than normally acid, indicating that the kidneys are disturbed by the emotions and that the body is off-balance.

The use of cider vinegar to combat the headache is by vaporising. Put equal amounts of water and cider vinegar in a small pan and boil slowly. When the fumes begin to rise, place a towel over your head and wait until the fumes are comfortably strong. Then take deep breaths of the mixture and inhale them for at least eighty breaths.

I know of numerous headache-sufferers who have found relief, and have never again used the normally accepted headache remedies.

Sore throats are also prevalent with many people, and here too cider vinegar with its germ-killing properties can help. Add a tablespoon to a glass of slightly warmed water and gargle. Three mouthfuls of the mixture should be used every hour and then swallowed after gargling.

A little nip of cider vinegar (two or three drops) in half a glass of water three times daily between meals, will help to strengthen the hardest working muscle in your body – the heart, for cider vinegar is a natural chemical that combines with heart 'fuel' to make the heart muscle even more powerful.

Our magic mixture can also aid and improve the digestion, help fight kidney-stones, combat arthritis and is a boon for constipation. Note that I say 'aid' and 'improve'. It is not a cure for any disease and, if you take cider vinegar, natural diets and plenty of the correct type of exercise should be carried out also.

The external uses of cider vinegar are worth considering – especially when it comes to healthy skin. In external use I have known cases of warts, corns and callouses being aided by cider vinegar; and burns and sunburns can be treated too.

With warts or corns, soak the parts involved in very warm water for about twenty minutes. Then dry and apply a full-strength cider vinegar using pieces of cotton. Leave on for ten minutes and then wash off with tepid water. Dry and then rub briskly with a rough towel. In the case of warts do not rub but pat gently dry.

The strong malic acid and the powerful enzymes in cider vinegar help kill off a common germ responsible for a number of scalp and hair conditions such as dandruff, baldness and itching scalp. Daily, moisten the scalp with finger-tips that have been dipped in a solution of one glass of tepid water to which you have added two tablespoons of cider vinegar. Before you shampoo or wash the hair pour on the scalp a cup of half-strength cider vinegar. Leave on for about three minutes and then rinse with tepid water.

I am certainly not suggesting that you try everything I have mentioned here all at one time. But get the cider vinegar habit. It really can be quite magical.

Foods to Avoid

There is quite a staggering list of foods to avoid in my fitness programme, so always look on the packet to see what you are eating.

To start with: refined sugar or refined sugar-products such as jellies, jams, ice-creams, candy, fruits canned in syrup, tapioca pudding, white rice. Avoid also all kinds of fried foods, saturated fats, and hydrogenated oils.

Coffee, strong tea, alcoholic beverages and tobacco, fresh pork and pork-products, lunch meats such as corned beef, and any meats, in fact, that contain sodium nitrate or nitrite are not recommended.

The list seems never-ending! Here are some more to avoid: smoked meats, sausage, ham, white flour products such as white bread, biscuits, buns, spaghetti, sago, pies, pastries, cakes and ready-mix products. Try also to do without drugs of all sorts, aspirins and sleeping-pills. A little exercise with my deep-breathing plan should help before going to bed. Also cut out, if possible, all kinds of tranquillisers and pain-killers.

Now for the foods you *can* eat that are free of toxins poisons and that will give you a clean blood-stream and a feeling of well-being, vitality and stamina.

In the meat section are roast beef, boiled or roast

chicken, roast lamb, grilled kidney, grilled liver, roast turkey. Fish (grilled, baked or steamed): cod, haddock, plaice, trout, tuna, white fish, sturgeon, sole, salmon, eel, roe, halibut, lobster.

Vegetables: tomatoes, runner beans, onions (raw or boiled), celery, mushrooms, lettuce, cucumber, carrots, cabbage, beetroot, peas, spinach, asparagus, greens, watercress, string beans, radishes, parsley, sprouts, green and red peppers, cauliflower, broccoli.

Fruits: apples, prunes, plums, pears, grapefruits, oranges, melons, figs, dates, apricots.

Do you know that your tongue never lies? It is often called the mirror of the body. The tongue reveals the amount of toxins that are stored in the body. When the doctor tells you to put out your tongue and sees it white-coated he knows at once the person is in a highly toxic condition.

The tongue is one end of a tube that is thirty feet long. People with heavily-coated tongues often have bad breath. A twenty-four hour fast will start to loosen the poisons in the body and the tongue will become more heavily coated. The fasting, you see, is now eliminating the poisons and cleaning the entire human pipe-system.

The characteristic formation of the tissues, especially of the internal organs such as the kidneys, liver, lungs and glands, is sponge-like. When the vital organs begin to fill up with toxins they sometimes become clogged with these sticky, slimy, decaying poisons, and the only way to purify yourself is to go on a natural cleansing diet.

I have always found that nature begins to heal the body if you 'stop eating foods that are full of these poisons, and concentrate on a system of internal purification by eating more raw fruits and vegetables, wholesome foods free from any form of the vicious toxic material that hardens the arteries and blocks them so that your blood cannot pass through. Hardening of the arteries does not happen overnight. It takes years to bring on this condition but it can start at an early age, even in young men between eighteen and twenty-eight. It has been revealed that everyone has a certain amount of hardening of the arteries.

Many products are made from refined white sugar and white flour. Over seven hundred chemical additives colour, preserve and stabilize these foods.

Perhaps the worst crime of all against us is that our food is sprayed with injurious insecticides. One of the deadliest is arsenic. No wonder so many of us are sick in health!

Eliminate as much heavy food as you can from your diet. Always remember, eating heavy foods does not produce physical strength. If you must drink tea, change to a herb tea. There are many first-class health drinks at health shops such as alfalfa, peppermint, and honey drinks and cocktail fruit-juices from fresh fruit.

When you make a salad-dressing really make it a meal full of energy and health. Add a health salad-oil (soya, sunflower, olive oil, safflower) or natural cider vinegar.

It will not be long before you feel more alive, better in health. Fruits and vegetables are the internal cosmetics which give you a glowing healthy skin.

ABOUT SACCHARIN

The trend towards slimming, especially among women, brings us to the subject of saccharin which is so much used by slimmers. American medical teams recently have formed the view that saccharin looks like providing an interesting chapter in medical history – and there has been talk in the States about it being banned.

This sweetener and sugar-substitute is certainly worth a mention in a book like this, for, like so many common everyday drugs, there is a big question-mark hanging over the wisdom of its use. There have been tentative suggestions that saccharin may form tumours in the bladder and uterus which may in some cases be malignant.

This has brought about some serious second thoughts about its widespread use in tea and coffee. Though it is true that saccharin has been used for over seventy years, the length of time by no means proves its innocence. Look at the facts. Saccharin is derived from coal-tar, which in turn is distilled from coal. While it may be up to five hundred times sweeter than sugar, it plays no part whatsoever in human nutrition. Saccharin is completely synthetic.

Diabetics, of course, use it as a sugar-substitute, as do overweight people and thousands of women who are anxious to slim. It is true that it might aid in that direction, but if the medical research is examined the situation looks rather different. Medical people accept, for example, that saccharin depresses the digestive processes, and thus strikes at the core of good nutrition.

Also, doctors have for many years said there can be harmful effects to the heart and the nervous system. It is claimed medically that the saccharin interferes with the formation of red blood corpuscles. However, warnings, notably from America, have not been heeded and saccharin is still very much in general use,

L

not only as a sugar-substitute but in soft drinks and confectionery. Cylamates, hailed as a safe substitute are now also under a cloud.

Yet again, the growing weight of medical opinion would appear to be turning against synthetic substances beside which there is such a big question-mark.

THE CONSTIPATION PROBLEM – AND ITS PREVENTION

Constipation, especially in chronic form, is aggravating and uncomfortable. It is an ever-present problem for many people in these hectic days. Like so many disorders, it can be prevented by the right sort of exercise and proper foods.

Everyone suffers from minor constipation from time to time. Nervous strain is probably the number one reason. A long journey, too, may upset the system. Constipation is something that should be high on your list of health-hazards to avoid. Distension of the lower bowel in chronic and unrelieved constipation can cause headaches, nervousness, mental confusion, backache, fatigue and several other distressing symptoms. Straining can cause other symptoms like hernia and haemorrhoids, while the digestion and absorption of nutrients can be impaired.

When it comes to the question of how often the bowels should move there is no set rule that everyone can follow in working out a schedule. With some it is two or three times a day; while with others it may be two or three times a week. The best plan is to try and adopt a toilet-routine with a visit at the same time every day – and do not allow anything else to interfere. This way you can train your bowels so that they will empty right on schedule. This is, of course, provided that you eat regularly.

Relaxation is another vital point. You should select a routine time when you will not be rushed. It can be done.

A brief word on the bowel function. When the food you eat has completed its journey through the small intestine, the waste that remains is dumped into the large intestine where it is processed ready for elimination. Most of the water in the waste is absorbed, and the remains are made up of firm solids. If, however, the waste remains in the large intestine for too long too much of the water is absorbed and that makes evacuating hard and lumpy waste a difficult matter.

Constipation causes hernia and that uncomfortable, painful, distressing ailment, haemorrhoids. The rule to remember here is that if the bowels are slow to move, do not try to force them, and always exhale when contracting the abdominal muscles. If you hold your breath while straining, a build-up of positive pressure in your chest and abdomen puts pressure on the big veins returning to your heart. If any of the veins have weak or defective valves they can become permanently swollen and enlarged.

What we eat is naturally very important. To some extent, all foods stimulate the bowels. Some are more stimulating than others. Raw fruits and vegetables, for example, assist elimination by contributing bulk-forming cellulose that retains water and sweeps clean the large intestine.

Good laxative foods are prunes, figs, raisins, dates, cabbage, beet, salads and apples. Also, whole-grain products. Try to get into the habit of eating two servings of fresh fruit and vegetables every day – raw when possible. What should be avoided are refined and artificial foods. Apart from lacking vitamin B, this type of food does not leave enough solid residue after digestion to retain water in the lower bowel.

A certain quantity of bran in the diet can be of assistance but there are some people who cannot tolerate pure bran, and they do better on a smooth rather than a rough diet.

It is best to be guided by your experience of the effect of the foods that you eat. Bran does not retain water as cellulose does, and an excessive amount might cause diarrhoea.

It is important to increase the number of friendly bacteria in the internal tract, and this can be done by eating types of yoghurt and drinking acidiphilus milk (from your health shop).

I am rigorously opposed to artificial laxatives. When you take a laxative you upset twenty-five feet of intestine, and if laxatives are taken regularly the whole intestinal tract will quickly fail to respond to the stimulation of ordinary food. In a nutshell, you eventually become wholly dependant on the use of laxatives. Frankly, it would not take long, through the improper use of laxatives, to cause the body great harm. The small intestines could be emptied too quickly, depriving the body of body-building nutrients by forcing the intestinal tract to eliminate partly-digested food. The best laxative, of course, is regular and sensible exercise which ensures that the body functions naturally and without need of artificial aids.

My advice to chronic constipation-sufferers taking laxatives is gradually to withdraw their use, at the same time increasing an intake of fruits, vegetables and juices. Drinking plenty of liquids is important. Especially recommended are fruit-juices, which contain organic acids that stimulate the internal tract. A good tip is to take lemon juice in warm water every morning before breakfast.

A powerful intestinal stimulant is coffee, but it can have harmful effects by lowering blood-sugar, constricting blood-vessels and over-stimulating the nervous system. If you have to drink coffee, drink it just before a regular toilet appointment – but never before retiring for bed.

Summing up, my main advice is to eat plenty of fresh fruit and vegetables, drink plenty of the right type of liquid, and never miss that toilet appointment on the mistaken pretext that there are more important tasks to attend to.

Slimming

A fat person is a jolly person, so they say. 'Laugh and grow fat' is an old adage, but the joke – and it is not very funny – is on them.

To be blunt, ignorance, laziness and simply over-eating are among the main causes of overweight; it is really a pitiful business. The only exceptions, and they are very rare, are those unfortunate people who suffer from improperly functioning glands. Your metabolism (the process whereby nutritive material is built up into living matter or broken down into simpler substances) is what regulates your body weight. Everybody has a different metabolic rate, and some fat people are simply unfortunate in that their metabolism does not cope with the quantity and type of food they eat. However, you will have learnt through experience just how much food your body can constructively use, and your aim should always be to eat just the food you need, as opposed to what you want.

The plush armchair, push-button existence that most of us lead today is of course no help. Labour-saving devices, and easy and ample transportation have, over the years, made living a simple matter with the abso-

lute minimum of exertion. And, further, there is just
no escaping the fact that the majority of people eat too
much. Many fat people do not really regard themselves
as lazy. They recline comfortably in armchairs, lie in
bed longer than necessary, curl up with a book and a
box of chocolates, or watch the latest entertainment on
television. Their slogan is ease. However, laziness and
disorganisation are not the only causes of overweight.
If you suffer from chronic overweight and are making
no headway in reducing it, you should consult your
doctor.

The best way to bring home the dangers and penalties
of being fat and overweight is to study the records
kept by insurance companies. These prove that fat
people die sooner than others and are not good
insurance risks; and the biggest cause for their early
deaths is heart trouble. Coronary disease, you do not
have to be reminded, is one of the biggest killers of
recent years.

You really owe it to yourself. Take a candid look into
the mirror and regard your expanding waistline. If
you keep on gaining weight at your present rate, what
will you be in five or ten years? And how long do you
think you will live?

The tragically sad and increasing number of deaths
from heart trouble has one big contributory factor. The
added weight and the greater quantity of living tissue
that has to be cared for place more strain on the heart.
The heart is a muscle that responds to proper training,
but in the case of overweights it has not been strength-
ened by exercise and is small in proportion to the great
bulk of flesh it must supply.

One must also consider that, if a person is overweight, the organs of the body must work that much

harder to perform their duties, so that the individual's resistance is lowered. This explains why a large number of fat people succumb to pneumonia and other illnesses.

There is no easy remedy like a vaccination to eliminate fat. The only absolutely straightforward cure is to strike a favourable balance between fuel-intake and energy expended. Obviously this means greatly curtailing the food eaten, or ensuring that sufficient exercise is taken to use all the heat and energy that food produces.

To my mind the answer lies in consistently and habitually utilising energy. Acquire immediately the habit of activity. Keep busy and exercise frequently. Resist long hours in an armchair with your eyes glued to the box and scorn that bad habit of using the car for short trips. You will surely find that as the amount of fat increases the desire for exercise decreases. So, make a stand, and establish a confident activity routine from this moment.

In another section, I have discussed at length the question of diet and food, and you must aim at cutting out the fat-forming foods. Principally, these are starches sugar and fried foods. Instead try to concentrate on these nutritious foods: any type of thin, clear soup and all sea-foods (except fried fish in heavy grease – it should be boiled or broiled). In the meat categories, lean beef and mutton are high on the list. Chicken and turkey are also good and, besides the fact that they do not produce weight, mutton, beef, poultry and fish are the four best meats for health and strength-building. Milk and fresh vegetables are also important foods, and cheese and fresh fruit can be included in the diet. When it comes to beverages, the inclusion of honey for sweetening is something I always encourage.

The exercises for overweight people are to be found elsewhere in this book. But this is the place for a quick word or two more about fat and the figure.

Fat enjoys a quiet and undisturbed existence, usually in the mid-section, hips and buttocks. Exercise to disturb that fat, cultivate a proper posture, and use massage. Posture is a definite essential. If you allow your body to droop, your back to become round, and your shoulders to slump, you will have a double chin, a hump at the back of the neck, an oversize seat and a slouching, dragging walk. So always adopt the right sort of carriage.

When tired, lie back for a moment and rest while alternately drawing in your waist as far as possible and relaxing. The same process can be adopted on side muscles, and you can massage your neck. Rub and knead here rather than simply sliding your hands over the skin. The same motion can be used on your face with the heel of your hand. This will chase the fat, smooth the face and prevent those wrinkles.

All other parts of the body, hips, thighs, seat and ankles, will respond to massage – always with the proviso that you have the muscle that exercise and activity will bring.

SLIMMING TO FITNESS

There is much emphasis in this book on correct eating. Its importance cannot be over-stressed. This is my own health-diet formula to lose weight and regain a firm, slim figure. It applies to both men and women. (You should consult your doctor before beginning a diet that will radically alter your eating patterns.)

Meats to choose from:

bacon, lean 2 oz; corned beef 4 oz; roast beef 4 oz; boiled
chicken 4 oz; lean ham 4 oz; roast lamb 4 oz; grilled
kidney 4 oz; grilled liver 4 oz; roast turkey 4 oz.

Fish to choose from: (fish must be grilled, baked,
steamed or boiled)

cod, haddock, plaice, trout, tuna, white fish, sturgeon,
sole, salmon, eel, roe, shrimps, halibut, lobster.

Vegetables to choose from:

tomatoes, runner beans, onions (raw or boiled), celery,
mushrooms, lettuce, cucumber, carrots, cabbage,
brussels sprouts, beetroots (boiled), peas, spinach,
asparagus, beet greens, watercress, string beans,
radishes, parsley, bean sprouts, green and red peppers,
cauliflower, broccoli.

Fruits to choose from:

apples, prunes, plums, pears, oranges, melons, figs,
dates, apricots, grapefruit.

The following drinks can be taken any time of the day:

health tea and coffee (black) – use a non-sugar
sweetener. Lemon and lime drinks, water, dietetic
squashes (sugar-free).

The following sauces and seasoning:

spices, pepper, paprika, salt, horseradish, mustard,
herbs and garlic can be used with any meal.

Over-eating is a slow killer. The average inactive person just cannot burn up the tremendous amount of food clogging the system, when unnecessary food is eaten daily.

DAILY MENU SUGGESTION

Morning

Glass of fruit juice without sugar, or cup of tea without sugar with one spoonful of milk. Boiled or poached egg with one slice of dry toast.

Mid-day

Salad consisting of one portion of meat, cucumber, raw or cooked tomatoes, beetroot, raw onion, one boiled or poached egg, one slice of bread, cup of coffee or tea without sugar with one spoonful of milk.

Evening

4 oz of corned beef, 2 oz of hard cheese, mushrooms, asparagus, string beans, white cabbage, 4 oz of tomato juice, one slice of dry bread or toast.

Supper

It is wise to finish the day with two fresh fruits, an orange and an apple.

You can prepare your own menu from the meats, vegetables, fish and fruits. You can choose four vegetables for each meal, but only one meat or fish dish. Two fresh fruits should be eaten once a day. Drinks can be chosen from the list and can be taken at any time of the day. Eggs and hard cheese can be included occasionally.

DIET FOR HEALTH AND NATURAL FITNESS

If you feel listless and lethargic, drowsy, only half alive, the chances are your eating habits are not what they should be. We are what we eat, and in these days when we are all under pressure it is a vital business indeed. Frankly, the average person does not really have the slightest idea of what he should build his body with.

The body is, of course, formed entirely from the food we eat and, to a large extent, disease becomes rife because people have not provided the body with the right sort of food to resist the disease. On another level, many people are bad tempered, worn out and exhausted simply because they do not know how to eat.

Today in fact our eating habits seem to be in a somewhat chaotic state. There are thousands of figure-conscious women who, bombarded by our twentieth century mass advertising media, are becoming fanatics about slimming diets. And through the same media we are all implored to buy a thousand and one food and drink items.

It is little wonder that today our eating habits are all wrong. Apart from too much misplaced eating, there is far too much overeating. The overeater could do well to remember that it is a medical fact that a person can live thirty days or more without a mouthful of food and still be reasonably strong at the end of that period.

Principally, my diet for a health-programme is one

of commonsense eating. Basically, eat and drink slowly and remember what foods nourish and build.

For building glands, the brain and the nerves, the following can be recommended: milk, fresh lean mutton, beef, poultry, fish or pork. These should be roasted, baked or stewed, not fried. In the same category come egg-yolks and cheese.

For purifying the blood and cleansing the system, we have fresh vegetables, lettuce, onions, peas, carrots and all kinds of fresh fruit. These foods all contain the greatest amount of minerals.

For strength and stamina – the bone and muscle-building foods – we have milk, bread, bananas, oats and most kinds of nuts.

Finally there are the solvents, which include grape-fruit, orange, pineapple and tomato juices.

Next, some main rules for eating. First and foremost, do not be governed just by what tastes good, and do not get into an eating rut. If you can operate a constantly changing menu of good-value foods, so much the better. Fatty, fried and greasy foods should be avoided, and condiments such as mustard, pepper, and sauces, ought to be restricted to the minimum, for they have no food value.

The advantages of eating slowly cannot be over-stressed. Get into the habit of chewing each mouthful well. The result will be an easier digestive process, saving energy. The same thing applies to drinking. Never gulp liquids. Sip them.

The advantages of eating in good clean surroundings are considerable, and the habit of sitting upright and straight at the table is another important point to remember.

Much has been written on the subject of eating and

diets, but the points I have mentioned are the basic ones.

After early morning exercise try this invigorating health-cocktail – a very natural rich source of the acid and potassium that the body needs for complete functioning:

Two teaspoons of pure apple cider vinegar.
Two teaspoons of pure natural honey.
Six ounces of water.

For breakfast, after that healthy beginning, a balanced daily menu could look like this: grapefruit, one egg (hard-boiled preferably) bread or toast, herb tea or coffee.

Then, remember that snacks between meals are a bad habit, try a salad with cooked vegetables for lunch.

Dinner should be the most important of the day's meals. After the tensions, pressures and strains of a working-day, it should be a contented, relaxed, happy meal. Try a fresh, raw vegetable salad, a protein food selection (lean meat, fish or poultry or cheese). And if you need dessert, a baked or stewed apple.

To start a health-diet, fast for twenty-four hours, taking only water and pure fruit drinks. I always recommend this to anyone if they are feeling under the weather. It really helps bring back your vitality and vital force.

Do not at any time drink tea or coffee. If you find it difficult to give up this drinking habit, buy herb tea and coffee from the health shop.

Again I repeat, while consuming the proper sorts of good food try and add variety; and at the risk of being repetitive, never overeat. Eat only when actually hungry and then make it a good wholesome assortment. And don't forget that early morning health-cocktail.

Conclusion

Any type of exercise that stimulates the circulation of the blood will contribute to improved health and longer life, and delay the ageing process. Endurance-type exercises, such as swimming, jogging, or bicycle-riding, are especially effective since they strengthen the heart muscle.

Weight-training,* in addition to improving your appearance, will help keep you youthful. There is now some evidence, for example, indicating that there might be a connection between lifting weights and the ability of the body to produce hormones that slow the ageing process. In a controlled study of seventy-five men between the ages of thirty-seven and fifty-four, at an American hospital, it was found that those who lifted weights showed an increase in the production of these hormones, while those who did not lift weights, but who exercised in other ways, showed a decline in hormone-production.

*Note; Weight-training, and any other vigorous form of exercise, should always be taken up in gradual stages, and under supervision. If you are ever in any doubt as to your health you should consult your doctor before setting out on a course of exercises.

My final words: this book was written for your health and well-being. You can, as I have stated, have good health and youthfulness at any age. Follow nature's rules; the only way to develop a body free of weaknesses and diseases and premature ageing. Systematic exercise and a correct diet free from toxic ingredients will give you many happy and healthful years of life.

Remember always – the greatest gift that you can have is health and strength. This book will start you on that road to a happier life.